TEACH

Marketing your
Small Business

TEACH YOURSELF

Marketing your Small Business

Ros Jay

Hodder & Stoughton

A MEMBER OF THE HODDER HEADLINE GROUP

Cataloguing in Publication Data is available from the British Library

ISBN 0 340 654740

First published 1996
Impression number   10 9 8 7 6 5 4 3 2 1
Year   1999 1998 1997 1996

Typeset by Transet Limited, Coventry, England.
Printed in Great Britain for Hodder & Stoughton Educational, a division of
Hodder Headline plc, 338 Euston Road, London NW1 3BH by Cox & Wyman Limited,
Reading, Berks.

CONTENTS

ABOUT THE AUTHOR

Ros Jay is a business writer and editor. After working as a PR manager she went freelance several years ago. Since then she has written press releases, annual reports, magazines and other literature for numerous companies, specialising in a clear, reader-friendly style. She also advises small businesses on PR and marketing.

Over the last few years Ros has written training manuals and guides on a range of subjects and she currently edits an internal newsletter for a large corporate client. She has co-written a book on how to plan and deliver presentations, *Effective Presentation*, and has written three books for Pitman Publishing/Institute of Management: *Low Cost Marketing, How to Write Proposals and Reports That Get Results* and *Build A Great Team!* She has also written *The Essential Marketing Sourcebook* for Pitman Publishing, which is one of the *Essential Business Sourcebooks* for which Ros is also series editor.

In addition to business topics, Ros has also written books on mythology, a subject in which she has had a lifelong interest, including *Teach Yourself Mythology*, published by Hodder & Stoughton in October 1996.

INTRODUCTION

If you were running a large business instead of a small one, you'd be employing several people – or even several departments – to look after most of the marketing. And as well as the staff on your payroll, there would be marketing consultants, advertising agencies, research companies, PR agencies, image consultants, direct marketing agencies... you name it, you'd have them working for you.

But you're lucky. You're not lumbered with some huge bureaucratic machine. You don't have to worry about keeping control of all those different people, all firing off in different directions. You're one of those fortunate people who run their own small business.

All right, so running your own business may sometimes seem like the short straw. You often have to work harder and longer than anyone else; there's no boss to call on for advice when you're not sure what to do; and sometimes it seems you have to run just to keep still. But believe me, when it comes to marketing, you really do have an advantage over all those huge companies.

Marketing is absolutely central to the business; it's the force that drives it along. It's not a job to delegate – it's too important. Of course, you can delegate marketing *activities*, but when it comes to planning and strategy decisions, they are far too important to hand over to someone else. Share them, certainly, if you have partners or fellow directors – it can only help – but don't give them up. Those poor MDs and CEOs of big firms are obliged to hand over all but the most crucial decisions. Whereas you get to keep a tight hold on the reins. Not only does that mean that you're far more in control of your business, it also means that you are better equipped to:

- adapt and change with the market
- see obstacles before they hit you in the face
- spot opportunities in time to make the most of them
- give a personal and individual service to your customers
- integrate different aspects of your marketing strategy

And one day, when your business has grown and you're employing hundreds of staff and several agencies, you'll understand your own company, and how to market its products and services, better than almost any other MD or CEO around, because with the help of this book you'll have had the best kind of marketing training of all.

1

WHAT IS MARKETING?

Many people interpret marketing as the promotional side of the business – advertising, exhibiting, direct mail, that sort of thing. Those are certainly all part of marketing, but it is far more than that. Essentially it is everything that drives the business along, and helps it – directly or indirectly – to grow. In effect, marketing is everything except for the manufacturing process, financial management, administration (including personnel), and management systems. These aspects of the business are driven by sales and growth. Marketing is the driver.

Let's take a simple example. Suppose you're a market trader; on the face of it, you might think that marketing your business was just a matter of setting up the stall and selling your goods. But when you think about it, there is a whole host of other decisions that will ultimately affect your profitability:

- At which market are you going to set up your stall?
- Which days will you run it?
- What products will you sell?
- How much will you charge for them?
- How will you let your customers know that you'll be at the market?
- How will you tell potential customers what you sell, where, when and at what price?
- How will you let people know where in the marketplace you are?
- How will you stop people buying from other stallholders instead of you?

- How are you going to make sure they remember who you are so they can come back and buy from you again?
- How will you behave towards your customers to make them want to come back?
- What can you do to make sure they recommend you to all their friends?
- What will you do if anyone complains to make sure they don't stop buying from you?
- How are you going to minimise the risk of their complaining?
- How will you know if there are other products they would like to buy from you if only you stocked them?
- If you stock items too large for the customer to carry home, are you going to deliver them? How?

All these are marketing decisions. And this is why marketing is so crucial to success – it's what your business is all about. Every decision you ever take that could change the number of sales you make or the value of those sales is a marketing decision. All the other business functions are there simply to support your marketing activities.

— Market driven or product driven? —

Marketing, as its name implies, is all about the market. And that's where your focus should be – on your customers and potential customers, and what they want to buy. This may seem ridiculously obvious, but huge numbers of small business people overlook this fact. It's usually *only* small business people that overlook it, because if you make this crucial error, you will never get to run a big business. In fact, before too long, you will find you're not running a business at all.

Focusing on the market is called being market led (or market driven). In other words you choose what route your business will take by following the market's needs and demands. The alternative to this is being product led, and this is a BAD THING.

There is a saying that illustrates this perfectly: losers set out to sell what they know they can make; winners set out to make what they know they can sell. There is only one reason for launching a commercial product or service: because there is a demand for it.

It can be very hard, for small business people especially, to be objective enough to see whether their product is truly in demand. This is one of the crucial functions of market research, which we'll look at in Chapter 2. You can become so attached to a business idea, you convince yourself that people want to buy it without ever making sure of your facts. It would be far easier if we were all like *Star Trek's* Mr Spock and viewed our own ideas with complete objectivity. The sad thing is, the majority of small business start-ups go bankrupt within three years (often taking the house, the family holidays and all the rest of it with them), and more often than not the cause is, at least in part, that the product or service was never going to sell but the owner couldn't – or wouldn't – see it.

I'll give you a real life example. I went to visit a small business a few years ago that was running into difficulties. It was run by two partners, both skilled craftsmen, selling good quality reproduction furniture. Or rather, failing to sell it. They had set up the business because they had been made redundant from a large local employer, and they thought they would much rather work for themselves. They were both good cabinet makers, enjoyed making furniture, so decided to set up a business doing that. (Alarm bells should have started ringing at this point – this is a classic example of product-led thinking.) When I met the two of them, they couldn't understand why their business wasn't getting off the ground. They were worried. They'd sunk all their redundancy pay into the venture, after all – renting a workshop, buying in equipment and raw materials, and so on.

I asked them if they could tell me what the problem was, as they saw it. 'Oh yes,' they said, 'We know what the problem is. We make big pieces of furniture – dressers and wardrobes and dining tables, and so on. The problem is that no one wants them. They all want small things like coffee tables and bedside cabinets instead.' These two were working really hard – like all small business owners – and wanted desperately to succeed, but they were losing their livelihood because they weren't focused on the market. If they had been – as you can see when you read it here in black and white – they would have switched to making coffee tables months before.

But don't let me depress you. The good news is that the viability of a product or service is not down to a whim of fate. The answers are all there in plenty of time for you to avert disaster – and often turn it into huge success. And by the time you reach the end of this book, you'll know where to find those answers.

EXERCISE

It's important to understand clearly this difference between market-led and product-led thinking. Just to make sure you've grasped it, have a look through the list of reasons below for starting a business or launching a new product or service. Identify which of them are market led (i.e. follow on from identifying a gap in the market) and which are product led (follow on from having a product or skill that you'd like to be able to sell).

1 There are lots of sporty, horse-riding and golfing people round here, so I reckon there are a good few fishing enthusiasts. But there's nowhere to fish. I wonder whether I could dig a lake in my field, turn it into a trout farm, and charge people for coarse fishing...?

2 I'd like to be my own boss, and I've never really used all those skills I picked up at art college. I really like painting on to china – maybe I should sell hand-painted china mugs.

3 I've invented an ingenious attachment for a food mixer, that grinds up the ends of soap bars and mixes them together into a fresh bar of soap. I could go into business selling it.

4 I've just noticed that the car roof-rack is constructed similarly to a sledge. I could make roof-racks that people can take off and turn into sledges for their kids in the winter.

5 I'd love to take the kids sledging but there isn't room in the car for a decent sized sledge. What I need is one that attaches to the roof – then I could strap their bicycles and tennis rackets to it as well.

If you found this at all difficult (and it can be quite tricky until you get the hang of it), have another look at the statements and ask this question of each one: what sparked off the idea – the *need* for the product, or the product itself?

Answers

1 Market led. The idea was sparked by the local people's need for somewhere to go fishing.
2 Product led. The starting point here is the desire to hand-paint on to china.
3 Product led. This is a product idea with no evidence of demand at all.
4 Product led. Just because something is possible doesn't mean it's useful. The starting point here is the technical feasibility of the project, not the need for the final product.

5 Market led. In this case, the whole train of thought begins with a need. The product is then designed to satisfy that need. Many of the most successful small business people start by identifying their own need for a certain product, and then establish whether other people share their view. A lot of aids for the disabled, for example, are thought up by disabled people who then go on to design and sell them.

The last two answers demonstrate that it's possible to arrive at the same product from two different directions. Of course, not every market led idea is guaranteed to work. You may have guessed wrong about the market need, which is why you have to do your research thoroughly as well. And some people whose ideas are product led happen to stumble across a gap in the market. But, once verified by research, a business based on a product idea for which there is no market need will fail, and one based on a market gap has the potential to succeed.

—— Marketing on a tight budget ——

As I said in the Introduction, you're going to have to do all your marketing yourself (you lucky person). And, of course, you'd like to do it all without spending any money. That's not quite possible - but you can do it far more cheaply than you might think. And you can make sure that all the money you *do* spend is a worthwhile investment that pays you back with interest.

In order to market your business effectively and inexpensively, there are a few guidelines to follow. These are general points that you can apply to every aspect of marketing as you go through this book, from planning and PR to direct mail and customer care. So here they are: the five rules of small business marketing.

1 Pretend you're a customer
2 Set objectives for everything you do
3 Make your mistakes in your head
4 Don't try to be too perfect
5 Know your limitations.

It's worth having a closer look at these five rules, because they are crucial to everything you do. They may not strike you instantly as major cost-cutting techniques, but I can assure you they'll save you more money in the long run than negotiating an extra five per cent discount with your key suppliers, or persuading your customers to pay you within seven days (although both of those will help, too).

Pretend you're a customer

Every time you are planning a new product or service, thinking of changing your prices, considering adding on extra services or making any other decisions that will affect your customers, put yourself in their shoes. Think, 'If I were a customer, what would I think about this? Would this be helpful? Would I find this irritating?' After all, the only person whose opinion matters in the end is the customer, so always imagine how your decisions will affect that opinion.

This applies to other exercises as well, like sponsoring the local school football team, or running an advertisement in the paper: 'If I were a customer, what would I think of a company that did that?' Or even, 'Would I know? Do I read that paper?' You need to think from the customer's point of view to be sure you're advertising in the kind of paper they read, or sponsoring the school they send their kids to.

And pretend you're a customer to analyse everything you *don't* do, as well as everything you do, in order to make sure you haven't missed out anything: 'If I were a customer, would I want the range to include a cheaper option?' Or 'Would I be happy with the delivery arrangements?' Or 'Would I know what to do if I couldn't get the thing to work once I got it home?'

Set objectives for everything you do

If you're not absolutely clear where you're going, you're unlikely to take the most efficient route to get there. Setting objectives helps you to focus on what you need to do to achieve them, and eliminate any wasted effort (for effort, read 'time and money').

Perhaps you've decided to mailshot all the customers who haven't visited your market stall in the last twelve months. Five per cent of them respond by ticking the box that says, 'yes please, phone us for a chat about your latest products'. Great! Or is it? I've no idea – what was your objective? Perhaps you could have designed the mailshot so that 10 per cent of them responded by placing an order. Or maybe what you really needed was to find out who to drop from your mailing list so you could save money on future mailshots. If you don't know exactly what your objective is, you are far less likely to meet it – and you could spend a lot of time and money in the process of missing it. And how will you know for next time what works and what doesn't if you don't know what you're trying to do?

Make your mistakes in your head

Mistakes can cost a lot of money, as you know. And you haven't got a lot of money (not to spare, anyway). So you need to minimise your margin of error in everything you do. The simplest and cheapest way to do this is to think things through. Obvious? Well, it should be, but it doesn't always happen. Let me give you a common example.

The local paper telephones you to sell you advertising space. You're aware that there must be plenty of potential customers out there who haven't bought from your market stall yet. So you say 'yes' (if you're a typical small business owner). Now, occasionally 'yes' is the right answer; but not as often as the local paper would have you think. This kind of reactive approach to advertising is a mistake. You should be starting at the beginning – 'How can I reach those potential customers?' – and thinking the problem through.

Ask yourself who these potential customers are, where they are, how you can best reach them: think each stage of the process through. Part of the thinking process includes pretending you're one of them – 'Where would I be likely to find out about this market stall? Do I read the local paper? What papers and magazines do I read? Where do I get together with other people like myself? Do we potential customers have anything in common – exhibitions we attend, trade press we read, places we visit?'

The final conclusion is not necessarily to advertise in the local paper. It may be to advertise in a specialist magazine, or perhaps not to advertise at all. Maybe you should be inviting them all to a factory tour, or sending out a mailshot, or attending an exhibition. There now – you've just saved yourself the cost of a wasted ad in the local paper, simply by thinking things through.

You don't have to think everything through on your own. Get together with business partners, friends or advisors if you can. Ask their advice, bounce ideas off them, think through problems together. Just make all the mistakes at the thinking stage, recognise them, and put them right before you go any further.

Don't try to be too perfect

This is a friendly, comforting rule. It's tempting to aim for perfection in everything, but it isn't always necessary. For example, suppose you want to know whether to introduce a new service to your customers. You know what it costs – the question is how many customers will want to use it? Having (by then) read Chapter 2, you decide to do some research to find out.

The thing about research is that (assuming you're doing it properly) the more you do, the more accurate your findings become. But how accurate do you need them? If you know the cost to you of this service, you will have calculated that you need, say, 20 per cent of your customers to use it for it to be worthwhile. In that case, don't waste time trying to find out *exactly* how many customers are likely to want the service, just do enough research to make sure that it will be more than 20 per cent of them.

This applies to a lot of aspects of business. Don't put time and money you can't afford into doing them better than you need to. Establish the standard you need to reach, and aim for that. To give you a slightly different example, you'll find out in Chapter 9 how to write a direct mail sales letter. You will almost certainly not learn to do it as well as the top experts who do it for a living. That's OK. You don't need to. You only need to do it well enough to bring in more business than you would otherwise, cost-effectively, and in a way that projects an appropriate image to your current and potential customers. You'll improve with practice. But if you start out trying to be perfect, you'll never get as far as mailing out the first letter.

Know your limitations

This complements the previous rule. You have to establish the standard that you need to reach. The previous rule says that you shouldn't waste time and money exceeding that standard; this rule says that you shouldn't waste time and money on falling short of the standard either. If you can't do the thing properly, don't do it at all. Get someone else to do it for you, or maybe drop the idea altogether, but don't kid yourself you're up to scratch when you're not.

I'm not talking about the early stages of the learning process – of course you might have to learn or practise to reach the standard you need. But once you have reached your full potential – at least for now – accept if necessary that you haven't reached the minimum standard.

This doesn't have to be a personal lack of skill. It could be a corporate lack of resources. Perhaps you really want to exhibit at a huge trade show at the NEC in Birmingham or London's Earl's Court. Lots of your bigger competitors will be there with expensive displays and glossy brochures. There are ways of making the most of restricted resources when it comes to exhibiting, as we'll see in Chapter 7, but there are limits. If you really can't match them cost effectively, don't try. Spend your money on a mailshot instead, or press advertising, or personal presentations to key potential clients.

Sometimes the inability to reach a certain standard is on a more personal level. Anyone should be able to learn the skills in this book, but we all have our own strengths and weaknesses, and you're bound to find some things easier than others. Occasionally you find a certain skill particularly hard to learn, and it may not be worth the time it takes. Perhaps when it comes to designing your own material on a desktop publisher, you just don't have an eye for layout. That's OK – but accept your limitations and hand it over to someone else, or at least ask for their input. Or maybe you find it incredibly hard to deal with complaints from angry customers. Once you've read Chapter 5 you shouldn't get too many of them, but perhaps you should have a system that (if you have the option) they are put through to someone else – your partner, your sales manager or whoever is appropriate.

Summary

There... that didn't cost too much did it? Those are the five basic rules of marketing your small business, and they all come free. Let's finish by recapping them, and then in the rest of the book we'll find out how to apply them.

1 Pretend you're a customer
2 Set objectives for everything you do
3 Make your mistakes in your head
4 Don't try to be too perfect
5 Know your limitations.

2
THE MARKETING PLAN

– Why do you need a marketing plan? –

It is unlikely that you would start cooking a meal that you didn't know the recipe for, or set out on a car journey without knowing the route you were going to take. But an awful lot of people run businesses without having a clue what their marketing plan is. They just make it up as they go along. It's rather like trying to drive from Land's End to John O'Groats with no map at all: 'Ah, Plymouth. I think we ought to be going up a bit and sort or rightish.' 'That's interesting; we're in Hull. Can you remember where that is? Isn't it a bit down from Durham? Maybe we should have gone the other way at Newcastle.'

Hopeless. The car may well give up the ghost before you ever get there. Even if you do make it, it will have taken ages, cost a fortune in petrol and accommodation, and taken a heavy toll on the car. And if it were a race, the competition would have been streets ahead of you, in every sense.

Running a business without a marketing plan is no different. You can't know what to spend your money on if you don't know what other demands are going to be placed on the budget later. You can't know where to focus your efforts if you don't know what the options are. And you can't know whether you're doing well or badly if you don't know what the standard is supposed to be.

Do you remember doing exams at school? You thought you'd done really well getting 68 per cent until you discovered that everyone else in the class had got at least 75 per cent. Well, marketing your business is easier than that: you get to find out before you start what standard you're aiming for. And as you go along you can keep assessing your performance against that standard. If you seem to be falling short, you can put in a little more work on this area or that to make sure you stay on target.

Why haven't you got a marketing plan already?

One of the main reasons why so many business people fail to draw up marketing plans is frighteningly simple: they don't know how to. This is often compounded by the fact that they don't want to admit that they don't know. Not because they are big-headed and don't like showing their ignorance, but because they feel it will give a bad impression. One of the most obvious people to go to for advice is the bank manager, but business people are understandably nervous of telling their bank manager that they don't even know what a marketing plan is, let alone how to draw one up.

If you recognise yourself in this at all, don't worry. For a start, you're about to find out what a marketing plan is and how to put one together. And for another thing, if you want detailed advice on your own plan, you can talk to your local enterprise agency (you can find out where they are from the National Federation of Enterprise Agencies; see 'Useful Addresses'). Many of them will give this advice free of charge.

——— What is a marketing plan? ———

A marketing plan is actually like a route map. It is a few, well researched pages that set out clearly:

1 where you are
2 where you are going
3 how you are going to get there (which includes what it will cost and how you're going to pay for it)

There is no exact formula for setting out the plan on paper. It's the information in it that's important, not the precise details of the layout (so long as it's smart, clear and easy to follow, of course).

The marketing plan starts now. If you are thinking about starting a business, or just in the process of starting, you need a marketing plan. If you have been up and running for a while without a plan, draw one up now, starting from wherever you are at the moment.

If you're wondering what the difference is between a marketing plan and a business plan, the answer is that the marketing plan is part of the business plan. To draw up a full business plan you will also need to include a financial plan, details of administration systems, manufacturing forecasts such as stock control, and so on.

Once the plan is completed, you will be able to use it to help you run the business. Indeed, you really must use it; you haven't got time to spare putting together documents that are going to spend the next five years stuffed away in the filing cabinet before eventually being consigned to the bin. Your marketing plan, on the other hand, is going to be your bible. You'll need to refer to it constantly to make sure:

- your performance is heading in the direction you planned
- you are on course to meet your targets and budgets
- you don't miss any marketing opportunities
- the competition isn't getting ahead

If any of the information in the marketing plan changes, you'll need to update it. It shouldn't be graven in stone. It's a flexible tool that is capable of adapting along with your business and your market. So hold regular review sessions – try once every two months to begin with, but more often if this time period seems too long for you. A word of warning, however: a review session is not an opportunity to lower your targets if things aren't going as well as you planned. The marketing plan should help you to work out *why* things have gone wrong, and then to find ways of putting them right again. Use it to revise your tactics to meet your original objectives. Don't adapt the objectives to fit your current tactics.

Let me give you an example of this. Suppose you run a local garage. You've been meeting your monthly sales targets for the last year, but for the last two months they've dropped. You go through your marketing plan and check off all the changes that could have contributed to this. There is only one factor that accounts for it: the new garage that's opened up a few blocks away. (Of course, you already thought that was the reason, but going through the plan made sure you weren't missing another, less obvious cause that also needed addressing.) You have two options when it comes to revising your marketing plan:

1 Lower your sales targets. After all, you can't expect business to be as good with a competitor just down the road;
2 Leave your targets where they are and change your strategy. Use your marketing plan to generate ideas about new places to look for customers, strengths to capitalise on, marketing opportunities to exploit and so on.

No prizes for guessing that the correct answer is the second option. So having established what a marketing plan is and how it should be used, the next question is how do you get it to give you all this useful information?

Drawing up the plan

There's really nothing difficult in putting the plan together; there's just a bit of work to do finding out all the information you need. But every bit of it is relevant to your business and your future success. And you already have a lot of the information, so it's just a matter of some hard, focused thinking. In fact, one of the most important things about both drawing up and using a marketing plan is that is makes you look at your business in a focused and clear way. And that, in itself, is one of the greatest abilities a business owner or manager can possess.

Identify the questions

To draw up your plan you need to ask a lot of questions. Then you need to answer them. Once you've done that, you have all the information you need, and it's just a matter of putting it down on paper in a sensible, logical order. So what are the questions?

Well, we need to go back to the original explanation of what a marketing plan is. There are three groups of questions, which will give you the following three groups of information:

1 where your business is
2 where it is going
3 how it is going to get there

Let's look at these three sets of questions one at a time. You'll know the answers to some of them straight away; the next section looks at finding the answers to the questions you don't know the answers to.

Where your business is now

This group of questions falls into four categories:

1 questions about the product or service
2 questions about the customers
3 questions about the business
4 questions about the competition

You want to find out all the information you can, and try to think of every possible question. The more work you do now, the more work – not to mention problems – you save yourself in the future. I can give you a list of questions, but bear in mind that it won't be exhaustive, and that there may well be some questions that are particular to your line of business. Write down all the answers you are confident you know, and save the rest until you've read the next section on researching the answers. As you go through the questions, you should see that you are building up a checklist of everything about your business, which will be invaluable for future planning, decision making and problem solving.

Questions about the product or service

You may think the answers to these questions are so obvious it's barely worth writing them down. But there are two reasons for going through the process. One is that you need a full marketing plan for outsiders to use – business advisors, bank managers you're trying to get loans from, and so on. And the other is that these fundamentals are often the areas that really need questioning if you run into problems later. And they are precisely the areas that people least often think to question. However, once you've built up this checklist for future use, you'll never be able to forget about them.

- What is the product or service? What is the product range?
- Where do the supplies/raw materials for it come from?
- What does it look like? Is there a choice of colours, finishes, accessories and so on?
- How is it packaged?
- How is it transported?
- Where is it sold?

- In what form does the customer receive it? (It could be bought ready to use, or it might need assembling, programming, defrosting or whatever.)

Questions about the customers

Don't guess the answers. If you don't have hard evidence, leave the answer blank until you have read the next section on research. If you really can't find the answer after that, there may be one or two questions which you have to answer on gut feeling – but aim to fill in more accurate answers at the first opportunity when you're reviewing the marketing plan later.

- Who are the existing customers? Businesses or individuals? What is their rough income? Age range? Where do they live? You may sell to more than one group, in which case you will have more than one answer to this question. For example, the local garage may have local business and private customers;
- How much are they prepared to spend? You know what they spend now (unless you're just starting up in a business with no direct competition), so include that. But do you know whether they might spend more?
- What do they like about the product/service? Not just in itself, but also the service they get, the price, the convenience, the aftercare, and so on;
- What do they dislike about the product/service? (Be honest.)
- What features do they like in this kind of product/service?
- What features do they dislike in this kind of product/service?
- Why should customers buy from you rather than from your competitors? In other words, what have you got that the competition hasn't? This is what is known as a Unique Selling Proposition (USP). Perhaps your product or service is the cheapest, or the highest quality, or offers a better guarantee than anyone else's, or can be delivered quicker?
- Who are the potential customers? Now is the time to start thinking about the customers who don't yet buy from you (if you're just starting up, this will be all of them). What type of people or businesses could you start selling to?
- How will they find out about the product/service? Where can you advertise or promote your products and services to attract their attention? Should you sell through retailers or agents, advertise in local or national media, attend exhibitions, mail customers direct,

promote through other businesses selling related products or services, or use a combination of approaches?

Questions about the business

Now is the time to answer questions about the business as a whole. One of the most standard and useful techniques for doing this is known as SWOT analysis (which is nothing like as technical and complicated as it sounds). Even if you are not yet in business but at the planning stage, you can still go through this process, and you should find it extremely helpful. SWOT is an acronym, which stands for:

- Strengths
- Weaknesses
- Opportunities
- Threats

And what you need to do is to list them all as they apply to your business. In other words, you're not looking at what you would like, or what you are aiming for, but what *is*.

EXERCISE

I'll give you a couple of examples so you're clear about the kind of answers you're supposed to be giving, and then you can fill in the blank SWOT table for your own business. After that, I'll give you a completed table, filled out with the kind of questions you should have answered in your own SWOT analysis. If you find you have missed anything out, go back and put it in.

Examples:

- Strengths – all your plus points. Good service, low prices, good management skills and so on;
- Weaknesses – all your minus points. Warning: fooling yourself can seriously damage your business;
- Opportunities – any gaps in the market, for example, or areas that you can exploit where the competition is weak;
- Threats – potential problems for the business such as strong competition or a shrinking market.

You've probably noticed that the strengths and weaknesses are internal factors about the business itself, whereas opportunities and threats are external influences.

Strengths	Weaknesses
Opportunities	**Threats**

Now take a look at the table below, and see if it prompts you into thinking of any additional points to include in your SWOT analysis.

Strengths	Weaknesses
Good technical/product expertise	Little technical/product expertise
Good staff availability	Poor staff availability
Highly motivated staff	Poorly motivated staff
Good market knowledge/experience	Little knowledge/experience of market
Good knowledge of competition	Little knowledge of competition
Broad customer base	Very dependent on one or two customers
Broad spread of skilled, capable staff	Very dependent on one or two key staff
Good reputation	Poor reputation
Well known	Unknown
Financially sound	Financially weak
Good location	Poor location
Low overheads	High overheads
High quality equipment and machinery	Equipment and machinery in poor condition
Flexible	Inflexible
Good internal communications	Poor internal communications
Good all-year-round business	Seasonal business
Up-to-date products/services	Product/services being superseded/ becoming obsolete
Opportunities	**Threats**
Competition is poor (perhaps in certain areas only)	Competition is strong
Competitor going bust	Competitors giving discounts/special offers
Market is expanding	Market is shrinking
Key exhibition coming up, ideal for new product launch	New legislation that may reduce market size or increase costs
New legislation that will increase market	Grants available to competitors
Grants available	Major customer going bust owing money
Better and cheaper raw materials available	Vital supplier going bust
Taking on promising new staff with valuable expertise	Risk of expensive legal action
	Key staff leaving

One of the great things about being a small business, which you may have noticed while doing this SWOT analysis, is that you probably have a lot of strengths that larger competitors may lack. It's much easier for you to be flexible, to give personal service, to keep prices down (because overheads are lower), to make decisions fast and so on. So next time your biggest competitor runs a national television advertising campaign, cheer yourself up by reading through your strengths and reminding yourself of all the things you can do that they can't.

Questions about the competition

This is crucial – and one of the most obvious areas, even at this stage, that you will need to revise from time to time to keep your marketing plan up to date.

- Who are your competitors?
- What extras do they offer?
- What are their strengths and weaknesses?
- What have they got that you haven't?

EXERCISE

Barclays Bank produce a useful brochure called *Setting up and running your business*. In it, they recommend you draw up and complete the following service/product comparison table comparing your service or product with your competitors'. There is no point in doing this unless you are going to be honest. One of the biggest traps many entrepreneurs fall into is convincing themselves that they are wonderful and the competition is useless. The failure to spot threats – which this inevitably leads to – can be enough to bring down the business. We can learn a huge amount from our competitors, but only if we accept that they have something to teach.

Go through the following Service/product comparison table, and fill out everything to which you already know the answer. After you've read the next section on research, come back to it and complete it.

Service/product comparison table

	Your product/ service	Competitor A	Competitor B
Price (standard for average product)			
Quality (good, medium, poor etc.)			
Availability (hours of work)			
Customers (business, general public etc.)			
Staff skills (good, medium, poor etc.)			
Reputation (good, medium, poor etc.)			
Advertising (where)			
Delivery (good, medium, poor etc.)			
Location (local, regional, national international)			
Special offers (if so, what are they?)			
After sales service (good, medium, poor etc.)			

One last thing about competition. Never forget the hidden competitor – the option of not buying at all. It's tempting to think that if there are, say, 5000 cars in your catchment area, and four other garages, that all else being equal you should attract around 1000 customers. But all the potential customers have the option of not using garages at all – and some of them will exercise that option. They will do their own repairs, or just drive old cars that barely go.

Where your business is going

These are your objectives. They include your sales forecast, but you should have other quantifiable marketing objectives as well. Only you know what these are but, to take the local garage as an example again, they might be such things as:

- To expand the business customer base to represent 30 per cent of turnover
- To increase the range of car accessories on sale in the kiosk
- To reduce the average time of a routine car service from eight hours to five hours

These objectives are obviously drawn up from the answers to the previous questions about where the business is now. For example, you want to expand the business customer base because you've discovered that business customers are more loyal, or that your competitors are particularly weak in this area.

The sales forecast
Only you can draw this up, but use the answers to the first part of the marketing plan, along with your experience, to tell you if there are reasons why the forecast should not be constant. Is your business seasonal? Are there opportunities or threats on the horizon that are likely to affect sales? Will you be launching new products, or taking on new sales staff? If you are starting up and this is your first sales forecast, allow for the fact that it is likely to take a while for sales to build up.

You can draw up sales forecasts on a weekly or monthly basis. Which is most useful? If sales are relatively constant and the market isn't changing too quickly, monthly will probably do. But in a fast changing market you may need to check your actual position against your target on a weekly basis. If you can't check your performance for a month you may have lost valuable time in adapting to the changes.

How your business is going to get there

This is your strategy. It is the means by which you intend to achieve your objectives and meet your sales forecast. List all the things you are going to do to make sure you arrive at the destination you are aiming for. The following list is not exhaustive, but it gives you an idea of the kind of options you have. You need to quantify all of them, and work out how long they will take and what they will cost. Otherwise how will you know whether you can afford them or have the staff to put them into operation?

- Redesign packaging – What are the objectives? What is the deadline?
- Attend exhibitions – How many? Which ones? With what objectives?
- Improve local press coverage – How many positive stories per year? Which papers?
- Expand database for direct mailshots – How? What size database? What specifications for the quality of the entries?
- Run mailshots - How many? To whom? To achieve what response? Converting into what value of sales?
- Advertise – Where? Aiming for what response?
- Improve links with other, complementary suppliers (to sell each other's products or services) – Which ones?
- Sell over the phone - How many calls a day? Leading to how many sales?
- Make sales visits – How many? With what result?

As I mentioned earlier, 'how you're going to get there' includes how you will pay for the costs of achieving your goals. So it's worth repeating that you will need to cost every one of these, and work out the time they will take to put into practice. The objectives must all be demanding but achievable. So how are you supposed to know what response you should expect to a mailshot? Well, apart from reading Chapter 9 of this book, the next section should help point you towards most of the answers. But if you're really stuck, make the best guess you can and then try it – and then revise your marketing plan to bring it into line with your experience.

Research the answers

So you've pages and pages of questions you still don't know the answers to. Now what happens? If you were a larger company you'd probably commission a researcher or a market research agency to find out most of the answers for you. Fortunately you can't afford that. Yes, fortunately – because you can't be tempted to spend good money paying somebody else to do what you can do perfectly well for yourself. There are three main places you can find the answers you're looking for:

1 ready-made information
2 your customers
3 other people

Ready-made information

There are all sorts of directories that will help you. If they are not in your local library they will be in your nearest main library. They include:

● Phone books, including *Yellow Pages* and the *Thomson Directories*
● Trade association yearbooks (you can find out who the trade associations are from the *Directory of British Associations*)
● *Kompass* (this lists British companies by industry, product, name and location – invaluable for finding out who your competitors are or for identifying new customers)
● *Municipal Year Book* (this is a directory of local authorities, with contact names)
● *The Retail Directory* (this lists buyers in large retail and department stores)
● *Marketsearch* (publishes around 20,000 market research reports - so you could find just the market research you need)
● *BRAD (British Rate And Data) Directory* (lists every newspaper and magazine in Britain that carries advertising – and gives you advertising rates and circulation figures).

There are plenty more directories – these are just some of the most useful – that you should find in any main library. You should also find the trade press for your industry a useful source of information. You'll find the relevant publications listed in *BRAD*, organised by industry.

Your customers

Before you even think of talking direct to your customers (which you should certainly do later), the first thing you should do is to look at your own customer records. Keeping thorough records is crucial, and the help it gives you drawing up your marketing plan is one of the many reasons why. Well kept records will tell you:

- which products or services your customers like best
- how many of them buy from you again
- how frequently they buy
- any seasonal fluctuations in buying patterns
- what they are prepared to pay (if you've ever changed your prices, the customer buying reaction should tell you a lot about how price sensitive your customers are)
- how promptly they pay
- what they complain about
- how quickly you resolve their complaints (yes, you should be keeping a record of this, but most small businesses don't: if you already do, you can feel pretty smug)
- how many of the complainers still buy from you afterwards

...to list but a few. Your own records really are one of the best sources of information you have; they are absolutely free; what's more, they are not available to your competitors. That should already have answered an awful lot of your outstanding questions. If you aren't yet running your business, don't panic. The other sources of information should give you pretty well all the information you need.

So far, you haven't spent any money at all. You've almost completed your marketing plan and all you've done is written out some questions and answers, done some hard thinking, and taken a trip to the library. OK, so maybe you've made a couple of phone calls. The other way of getting information out of your customers is blindingly simple – you ask them. And this is where you may have to spend a little money – but very little. If you're still in the process of setting up the business, or if you're already running it, you can also apply these techniques to approaching potential customers. There are three main ways to ask your customers for information:

Chat informally while you're doing business with them: 'By the way, we were wondering whether it might help our customers if we installed a car wash. What do you think?'

- *Plus points* – This approach is cheap, and it can generate some valuable comments and suggestions that wouldn't come out of a preset list of questions;

- *Minus points* – You can't ask more than one or two questions like this; the customer won't want to hang around chatting for hours. It's difficult to be scientific about the questions, and therefore confident of the results, because you tend to word the questions slightly differently each time, or even ask different questions entirely. It's hard to build up a sample large enough to be reliable;
- *Verdict*: This is useful if you're looking for suggestions and ideas, or answers to a single question, rather than trying to research several areas of your business.

Telephone them: 'Hello Mrs Wheeler, it's Pat from Auto's Garage here. We're trying to find out how we can improve our service to our customers. I wonder if you could spare me a couple of minutes to answer a few questions?'

- *Plus points* – You can make sure you ask everybody the same questions, and there's an opportunity to ask for suggestions and ideas as well;
- *Minus points* – this is a fairly time consuming approach, and can be costly in telephone bills if you're hoping to build up a large sample;
- *Verdict*: This approach is best when you only need to speak to small numbers of people, especially if you want to quantify the number of people giving each answer but also want some freeflowing conversation to generate ideas.

Send them a questionnaire. This doesn't have to be expensive to print, or you could even generate it on a word processor. You can hand it to customers who visit, or send it out with deliveries or bills, to save postage.

- *Plus points* – this is by far the most cost-effective way to produce large numbers of responses, and therefore come up with more statistically reliable results. You can make this method anonymous, which can lead to more honest replies;
- *Minus points* – Although you can keep the costs down, you can't do this for nothing. You also need to design the questionnaire quite carefully to be sure that the questions are clear. Otherwise the answers won't tie up. A badly designed question that no one understands could evoke responses ranging from 'senior buying executive' to '3' (I've seen this happen) – how are you going to add up those sorts of responses? Speaking of which, analysing answers to written questionnaires takes time – another minus point. And the response rate can be very low – as little as 1 per cent is not uncommon - so you need to send out a lot of them;

- *Verdict*: Use this approach if you want to know a lot of people's answers to the same list of questions.

For all these approaches there are a few vital guidelines to follow:

- Think hard about what you want to know, and then decide which questions will best elicit the information you want;
- If you're asking everyone the same question, ask them *exactly* the same question, otherwise you won't be able to add up the answers accurately;
- Don't weight the questions. If you ask people 'Don't you think it would be useful if we installed a car wash?', most of them will say yes. Instead, try something like 'We're considering whether it would be useful if we installed a car wash. What do you think?'
- Be unambiguaous in your questions. If you ask someone 'Do you spend a lot of time driving the car?' they may have a different view from you of what constitutes 'a lot'. They might think three hours a week is a lot; or that fifteen hours a week isn't much at all. So ask them 'How many hours a week do you spend driving the car?'
- If you're relatively inexperienced at producing written question-naires, ask multiple choice questions with tick boxes for the answers. That way you'll be able to analyse the answers much more easily;
- As a general guide, keep telephone interviews down to five or, at the most, ten minutes. Written questionnaires should take no more than five or ten minutes to fill in; the longer they take the less likely people are to bother. Experts in market research will tell you that you can sometimes make them much longer – and so you can, if you're an expert and know all the exceptions to the rules. But we don't, so we won't try it;
- People are much more likely to respond to postal questionnaires if you give them a return envelope with the address already on it – even if they have to find a stamp for it themselves.

Other people

There are several categories of people other than customers who you can get information from:

- Suppliers: many of your suppliers will have plenty of research information about their products or services which they may be perfectly happy to talk about. They may also supply your competitors – while it may not be ethical to ask for confidential information, they will probably tell you whether you're buying more or less from them than others, or whether you are receiving more complaints relating to their supplies than other companies in the industry are. And the better your relationship with your suppliers is, the more they are likely to tell you;

- Your competitors: fair enough – if you go to them direct, they may not invite you in warmly for a glass of wine and a chat. But there are other ways of finding out about them. Get hold of all the information you can from them: ring them and ask for their annual report, quotes, brochures and so on. If your address is a giveaway, use a different one if you can, or ask a friend to ring for you. It can feel uncomfortable doing this, but you're only asking for publicly available material, and if they have any sense they'll be doing the same to you. Make a note of their efficiency, friendliness on the phone (it is better to make calls yourself if you can), and the speed of their response. Visit their stands at exhibitions, collect their point-of-sale material from shops, and read everything you can find about them in the local, national or trade press;
- Advisors: talk to your local enterprise agency. Much of their help is free, and they can point you towards all sorts of other sources of information as well.

Finalise the plan

You're now ready to fill in the rest of the answers, making informed guesses where you have to (but only where you really can't avoid it). Once you've done that, you've got your marketing plan. It's just a matter of putting it down on paper in the right order. You're aiming for a document that is somewhere between two and ten pages long, depending on the complexity of your business, and the number of markets you're selling into (such as the garage that has both business and private customers). If you want to know whether you should divide up your target markets like this or whether you should group them all together, it's simple: if you treat them differently – in terms of targeting promotions, pricing or anything else – you'll need to separate them out on the marketing plan. If you sell to them all in the same way and via the same approaches, group them together in the plan.

The marketing plan

I'll summarise by recapping the main points of the marketing plan.

Where your business is now:

1 The product/service
2 The customers
3 The business
4 The competition

Where your business is going:

5 Objectives
6 Sales forecast

How your business is going to get there:

7 Marketing strategy

Did it work?

Well done – you've got a marketing plan. And if you've put it together properly, it won't be long before you start wondering how you ever managed without it. But hang on... how do you know if you've put it together properly?

The first thing to do is to show it to other people. If you're running the business with someone else, you'll already have been talking it through as you went along. But either way, take it to someone who you trust – not just someone who is a good judge of these things, but also someone who will tell you straight if they think it's unclear, not specific enough, incomplete or unrealistic. A friend, perhaps, or your bank manager or accountant. Show it to three or four people if you're lucky enough to know three or four who fit the bill.

After that, the real test of the plan will be when you start using it. Any flaws or weak spots will show up at your review sessions, and you'll have the chance to remedy them. You're not stuck with your mistakes. And the more time passes, the more accurate your plan will become. But if you've followed the guidelines in this chapter, and shown the final plan to a couple of useful critics, you won't have gone far wrong.

And finally, a marketing plan, however good, only works if you use it properly. Use it as a continuous checklist of what you should be doing to maximise your company's success. Use the SWOT analysis to generate ideas; keep asking yourself 'How can I make more of these strengths and opportunities? How can I minimise the potential damage from these weaknesses and threats?' Every time you meet your objectives or your strategy targets, ask 'What challenge can I meet next?' and let the marketing plan give you the answer.

The hard work is in putting the plan together – hard, but by no means impossible, and it should be interesting and fun with it. Now it's completed, the plan will take over the hard work from *you*. The plan will be asking you the questions, and giving you the answers. All you have to do is keep the information up to date, and learn to listen to it.

3

IMAGE

Every time our customers see us, speak to us or hear from us we send them messages about our business. Our advertisements, press coverage, sales letters and brochures not only tell them where to find us and what we're selling, but also give them dozens of other messages whether we like it or not – such as what quality our products or services are, whether or not we're a friendly company, whether we're stuffy, modern, efficient and so on. Even our company van, our answerphone message and the clothes they see us in will influence their view of the company.

People see businesses and organisations as personalities in their own right. For example, most of us see Rolls-Royce as an exceedingly respectable, upper-class company with an innate sense of style. We see Greenpeace as a young, somewhat radical, highly principled organisation, that occasionally shows the tendency of the young and principled to rush headlong into things. Virgin is ambitious and intelligent, and loves a challenge.

These are all human characteristics. And that's how we view businesses – we anthropomorphise them. And that's what your customers and potential customers will do to your company – they will unconsciously give it a character. And they will judge it on every little thing, just as we all form opinions of people based on tiny details as well as the overall picture ('I thought he was very nice, but did you notice the way he spoke to his kids?' 'She was sweet, but what a peculiar laugh!' 'I do like him really, but I've never forgotten that time he was really offish with my parents').

You need to decide exactly what personality suits your company, and then make sure that you project that image in every little thing you do. That's what this chapter is all about: how to choose the right image, and how to project it.

────── Choosing the right image ──────

So what is the right image for your company? You need to think in terms of personality. In many ways this is easier if you're running your own small business, because some of the characteristics are likely to be your own. For example, if you're supplying and maintaining houseplants to local offices, and you have a bright, friendly, chatty personality, your clients are likely to associate those characteristics with your business as well as with you personally. Some business owners maintain this personal/corporate image even when they grow larger. Look at the description of Virgin, above. I could just as well have been describing Richard Branson rather than his company.

But even if you do overlap your company's image with your own, you still need to think it through consciously to make sure it really happens, and to make sure it is followed through by any other staff you take on to represent your company. Not to mention the fact that we all have aspects of our personality that we don't want to show through – such as our depression when we realise we're not going to get as big an order as we hoped this time.

EXERCISE

In a moment, we'll find out how to choose an image for your company. But first, here's an exercise focusing on other companies that will help when you come to think about your own business.

Below is a list of organisations. Go through it, writing down a few words that describe the way you see each organisation's personality – along the lines of the earlier descriptions of Rolls-Royce, Greenpeace and Virgin. The last three spaces are blank for you to write down the names of three organisations that are local or particular to you. There's no right or wrong, because the question is not how do they

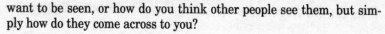

want to be seen, or how do you think other people see them, but simply how do they come across to you?

1 Microsoft

2 British Rail

3 The Red Cross

4 Midland Bank

5 Lloyds Bank

6 BBC

7 ITV

8 Your local supermarket

9 One of your local independent shops (such as the local newsagents)

10 The trade association for your industry – if there isn't one, any trade association or business institute you have had dealings with

You'll notice that some of these examples are of organisations that do virtually the same thing – such as the BBC and ITV. But most people would give them slightly differing characteristics. This exercise is quite fun to do; try going through the list with friends or colleagues to see how similar everyone's answers are. You'll normally find a slight variation but not a marked one, unless someone has had a particularly memorable experience, either good or bad, with one of the organisations on the list.

The three ingredients

You'll probably have noticed with the exercise you've just done that it's quite easy to come up with the first three or four words to describe each organisation, and then it becomes harder to think of them. There's a reason for that – customers and potential customers can't really take on board more than a few key characteristics, because they aren't consciously thinking about it; they are just absorbing these messages subliminally. So you need to find the best three or four words to describe your company's ideal image. When you're deciding what image will best suit your business, there are three factors to take into account:

1 your personal image
2 your product or service's image
3 your customers' image

Once you've found the key words for each of these, you can look for the overlaps, or the strong points, and merge these three factors to give your business one clear personality that encompasses you, your products and your customers. We'll look at each of these in a little more detail.

Your personal image

This is the one factor you could leave out, particularly in a larger business, but it's important to include it if you have a lot of personal contact with your customers, as most small business people do. You need to be sure that you focus on the most positive aspects of your personality, of course, and the ones that come across to other people (which are not always the ones you think they are).

What you need is for two or three exceedingly honest colleagues or friends to tell you what your most obvious characteristics are. For those of us not blessed with as many as two friends who are that honest, I suggest you enrol a few more people to help you, and ask them to give their opinion anonymously. Get them all to write down on a blank piece of paper the key words that they feel describe you, and shuffle them so you don't know who has written what. If you are in business – or just starting up – with other people, you should try this on each other and see where you can find characteristics that are common to you all. Now draw up a list of about four to six words that come up most often (people may not use exactly the same words, but you'll know whether they mean the same thing. Here are some of examples of what your final list might look like:

- outgoing, ambitious, kind, organised, dynamic, inventive
- respectful, quiet, hardworking, intelligent
- enthusiastic, perfectionist, friendly, efficient, honest

The reason for approaching this aspect of your image from this point of view (rather than thinking up from scratch the characteristics you would like to put across), is that you are going to find it immensely difficult to spend your entire working life pretending to be someone else whom you've invented. Why not do it the easy way? The characteristics of the other two factors – the product or service and the customer – can shift the emphasis, but within an achievable range. For example, your profile might describe you as friendly. That's unlikely to be a bad thing, but there are different types of friendliness. There's the outgoing chattiness that you might want to portray if you were running a pub, or the polite but not over-familiar friendliness that you would employ if your customers were all traditional solicitors.

So you can adapt these characteristics, but it's easier to focus on characteristics that you have in some measure to start with. And remember, you're not trying to come up with a new image for yourself; you're looking for a clear, recognisable image for your business. But it has to be one that *you* aren't going to inadvertently contradict every time you meet a customer.

Bear in mind that even the most negative seeming characteristics have positive aspects: you can translate stubborn into determined, careless into tolerant, pushy into enterprising and so on.

Your product or service's image

Once again, you need to produce a list of about four to six descriptive words. These must describe what the product or service is, not what you would like it to be. You will probably find it much easier to get an objective view of this if you ask someone outside the business – a friend or ex-colleague – to give you their view. Ideally, ask the bunch of friends who wrote down your own most obvious characteristics to describe your product or service as well (if you're still speaking to them). Once again, pull out the words that crop up most frequently to form the final list.

There are a couple of points to make about this section of the process. First, you may find it harder to choose personality-type words. There's a tendency, especially with a physical product rather than a service, to veer towards words like 'quality' or 'durability'. It's better to avoid this tendency if you can, but don't get too hung up on it; this only represents a third of the ingredients for your final image recipe.

Second, you may be wondering what you're supposed to do if you have a varied range of products or services, all with different characteristics. This is where there's an even bigger advantage in using outsiders to make an assessment for you – they'll be less confused by this than you will. Think of Marks and Spencer. Their two main ranges of products are food and clothing, although they also sell gifts, household items and so on as well. But there are personality descriptions you could attach to all of these collectively such as reliable, easy to get on with, or no-nonsense.

Your customers' image

You can probably do this part of the exercise yourself, or together with any business partners. If you are just starting out, you will obviously have to list the characteristics of your target customers rather than your actual customers.

List the characteristics that are shared by the bulk of your customers collectively; obviously there will always be a few individual exceptions. But you'll probably find that most of your customers are traditional, or young, or adventurous, business-like, unconventional, stylish, or whatever. Again, come up with a list of up to six traits.

Putting it all together

Finally, you need to bring together your three lists, and find the words that crop up on all three. As we saw before, there's no point in having loads of aspects of an image to put across – the customer will just be confused. So you want to focus on only two or three. You may be surprised at how much overlap there is between the three lists. This is because most people have at least an overlap between their own personality and the product or service they choose to sell. The product, in turn, while not necessarily being a perfect personality match with the customer, is nevertheless likely to appeal to customers with similar characteristics. It would be really surprising if a staid, old-fashioned, reserved person decided to go into business selling novelty exploding golf balls and then found that all their customers were eco-friendly academics.

To take an example, the lists of a business selling pot plants to offices and maintaining them could look something like this:

- Personality: bright, friendly, chatty, efficient, easy-going
- Product/service: fresh, friendly, welcoming, smart
- Customers: business-like, smart, efficient, friendly, caring (remember, these are specifically business people who think it worthwhile spending money on plants in the office)

There are quite a few overlap points here: friendly (which crops up three times), efficient (twice), smart (twice). What's wrong with that as a company image: friendly, efficient and smart. If you don't have three precise overlap words, you should find some close matches, such as friendly and welcoming, or efficient and business-like. If you only have two words on your final list, that's fine.

Corporate identity

Many people confuse corporate image and corporate identity. Identity is the visual aspect of your image – your logo, house colours, typefaces and so on. In other words, the bits that appear on your letterheads, business cards, brochures and so on. If your corporate image is your personality, your corporate identity is the way you dress. Important, but not the whole story.

However, you want your appearance to suit your personality. One of the most expensive things you can do when it comes to your company image is to contradict yourself. If you spend money on sending out signals that say 'we're friendly, efficient and smart' and then send out letterheads that carry the message 'we're slapdash', you've wasted your money completely.

Your company name

So having chosen your image, you need a corporate identity that matches it. If you're just setting up your business, this will include choosing a name for it. Use your image to define your choice of name: list all the names you can brainstorm, and then find the one that best suits your list of 'image' words. Suppose your choice of names for the pot plants company includes:

- Pat's Plants
- Greenfingers
- The Office Plant Company
- Pick of the Bunch

Choose the name that sounds the most friendly, efficient and smart. In this case, I'd say The Office Plant Company. It gets on with it, and says exactly what it is – an efficient, smart thing to do. There's no need to be clever with a company name, and in fact if you're too clever people won't be able to work out who you are and what you do.

Consider whether potential customers will come to you, or you'll go and find them. In a business with a few lucrative clients, whom you contact directly, it matters less whether they can tell what you do from your company name, because you'll be there to explain it to them. But if they are going to come to you, your name needs to tell them they've come to the right person. When they're looking through the *Yellow Pages*, 'Smith & Jones Plumbing' will mean a lot more than just 'Smith & Jones' or 'Radfix'.

Your logo

Once again, your logo should reflect your image. If you do go into business selling those novelty exploding golf balls after all, you'll probably want a humorous logo. If your image is staid and respectable you'll want a simple image, or plain lettering with no symbol or picture at all. Your friendly, efficient and smart Office Plant Company will want a logo to match. Either lettering only, or a simple leaf design, perhaps. A detailed drawing of a palm, for example, will look too confused to be efficient, and too fussy to be smart. Have a look at the two versions below, and you'll see what I mean.

Lettering

The rules for lettering are really similar to the rules for logos (if you have only words in your logo, they are exactly the same thing, of course). Most fonts (the collective name for a group of typefaces – the bold, italic, capitals and so on all grouped together) give a clear image of being smart, down-to earth, old fashioned, jazzy or whatever. Pick one that matches your chosen image. Here are a few options for The Office Plant Company. I think the last one is the most friendly, efficient and smart.

THE OFFICE PLANT COMPANY

The Office Plant Company

The Office Plant Company

The Office Plant Company

The Office Plant Company

Colours

Colours are intriguing. I'm always fascinated by how much your choice of company colours says about your business. You can't avoid it. Every colour means something. But don't start to panic about the hidden messages you're unwittingly sending out; it's not hard to work out what they mean once you think about it (what interests me is *why* they mean what they do – but fortunately we don't need to know the answer to that in order to use them).

The fact that colours mean so much shows that we do all make judgements about organisations based on their corporate colours – we just don't realise we're doing it. All we need to do is to listen to our own unconscious reactions to other businesses and we'll learn everything we need to know about how to send out the right messages ourselves.

I'll give you a few examples of colours, or groups of colours, and you should start to see what I mean.

- Dark colours tend to be smarter, and more traditional;
- The really smart, most traditional colours of all are the colours that you would associate with a Victorian leather and mahogany study: deep green and burgundy;
- Yellows introduce a light, cheerful and even fun element – more suitable for selling Christmas gifts than residential homes;
- Contrasting colours (such as red and green) are more cheerful and modern than co-ordinating colours (such as royal blue and rich purple). You could use contrasting colours to sell kids' toys and co-ordinating colours to sell elegant and classy picture frames;
- Reds (apart from very dark or muted shades) are dynamic – better for selling sports equipment than aromatherapy oils;
- Green and brown together give a rustic, homespun impression – good for handwoven rugs but perhaps not for fax machines;
- Different shades of the same colour can give very different impressions – a deep traditional sea-green could be excellent for selling smart briefcases – mid-tone greens seem to be reserved (for some reason) for estate agents and environmental organisations;
- Pastel shades can be quite feminine and less business-like. Better for a boutique than an office stationery supplier or a bulldozer manufacturer.

Some products suggest particular colours. Handmade floor tiles seem to suggest a variation on terracotta, and The Office Plant Company suggests a green colour scheme; probably a dark, slightly bluish green as this is more smart and efficient than yellowish-greens or pale green.

If you're in the export business, by the way, check what your house colours mean in other countries. For example, black and red are associated with evil spirits in Brazil, and white means death in Japan.

If you can afford it, you might consider using two colours together. I've already mentioned the effect of using contrasting colours and co-ordinating colours. Sometimes you can put across two messages, one with each colour. But be careful - people won't take in two completely different messages; they must be similar but one can add to the other. You need to make one the main colour and the other the supporting colour.

To give you an example, I worked with a company that wanted to pep up its image. It wanted to come across as a company with traditional standards and values, but without an old-fashioned attitude. Its colour had been a plain purple. We shaded this down into a deeper, smarter, traditional deep burgundy to give a more traditional image, and then added a light grey, which is a modern colour, but not a jazzy one. The burgundy was the main colour, and the subtle grey – not overused – co-ordinated and added a less old-fashioned feel to the overall effect.

Projecting your image

The most important and obvious part of projecting the image you've chosen is to *do* it. What I mean by that is that as well as sending out your subliminal messages on all your advertising, press stories and so on, you (and all your staff) also need to *be* your image. Be friendly, efficient and smart, or whatever it is that you've picked. Otherwise you not only waste your money and cloud your image, you also make a fool of yourself. A prime example of this would be an advertisement for an educational establishment saying 'Nothing gives you such a good start in life as a colledge education'.

Make sure that you project your corporate image in everything you do, and use your corporate identity on everything your customers ever see. That way, they'll get the message loud and clear.

EXERCISE

You can project your image, and your corporate identity, in more ways than you might imagine. Work through the list below, and under each heading list all the things you can think of that send out messages to your customers or potential customers. So, for example, under 'stationery' you would want to include letterheads, business cards and so on. And don't forget the non-visual messages as well, such as the manner in which you answer the phone, or the efficiency of your delivery service.

1 Personal presentation

2 Stationery

3 Printed materials (other than stationery)

4 Packaging

5 Telephone manner

6 Customer care

7 Selling

8 Presentations

9 Public relations

10 Advertising

11 Exhibitions

12 Company vehicles

It would be quite impossible to list every single sign you could be sending out. But I'll go through the exercise and list several under each heading; you may well find there are quite a few you hadn't thought of.

1 Personal presentation

- style of dress
- tidiness
- body language
- promptness

2 Stationery

- letterheads, compliment slips
- business cards
- envelopes
- invoices, statements, delivery notes

3 Printed materials (other than stationery)

- sales brochures
- price lists
- proposals
- signs
- instruction leaflets
- style and quantity of wording
- how well written

4 Packaging

- visual design
- how easy it is to undo
- how well it protects what's inside
- the information it carries

5 Telephone manner

- what you say when you answer the phone
- speed of answering
- friendliness
- efficiency, such as in message taking and ringing back

6 Customer care

- method and speed of handling complaints
- degree of familiarity with customers

- frequency of contact with customers
- after-sales service

7 Selling

- prices
- style of selling (such as soft sell or hard sell)
- frequency of approaches
- amount of time spent with customers

8 Presentations

- how promptly they start
- how well planned and organised they are
- what information they include, and how much of it
- how formal or informal they are
- any presentation materials or handouts
- quality and style of visual aids

9 Public relations

- press releases
- media interviews
- size and type of events held
- how well organised events are
- local sponsorship (or absence of it)

10 Advertising

- where you do it
- size of ads
- wording of ads
- black and white or colour
- design of ads

11 Exhibitions

- where you exhibit
- size of your stand
- design of display
- printed support materials
- amount of information available
- how inviting your stand is
- demeanour of stand staff
- your pre-publicity

12 Company vehicles

- type of vehicles
- how clean they are
- how considerate the drivers are

Yes, all these things tell people something about your business. Make sure it's telling them what you want them to hear. Don't panic at the length of the list. You're probably getting an awful lot of these right already without even realising you're doing them. And some of them may not apply to your business anyway (perhaps you don't use a company van, or use packaging materials). And anyway, we'll be going into most of these areas in a lot more detail later on. But this exercise should give you an idea of how many signals we send out all the time, which is why it's so important that they are clear and consistent.

Keeping the cost down

The best way to minimise costs is to be consistent. If you aren't fighting yourself, by muddling your corporate identity or behaving in a way that contradicts the image you want to put across, you can express yourself clearly with little cost and effort. Your company image is not an expensive thing to develop. As we've already seen, you'll acquire an image whether you like it or not – that comes for free. You're just making sure that the one you acquire is the one you want.

When it comes to logos, lettering and so on, you can't manage without stationery, or display boards if you're exhibiting, or sales brochures. So you're not adding to the expense, you're just making sure that all the money you were spending anyway goes on the right colours, typefaces and so on.

Printing

There are a few tips worth mentioning when it comes to printing stationery, business cards and so on.

Paper There are a lot of expensive, fancy papers on the market – marbled or watermarked or textured or whatever. You don't need them. Just make sure that the paper you use is of a quality that matches your image. If you're selling an expensive product, don't send out letters on flimsy, cheap paper. Your printer can advise you on this if you ask.

Colours You can save money at the printers in several ways when it comes to printing colours:

- It costs about the same whatever colour you print in – so it doesn't have to be black. If you're printing quite a lot of solid text, for example in a sales brochure, there's a tendency to think that it has to be black. It's true that it should be a dark colour or it will be harder to read, but if your house colour is dark anyway, you can print in that and save the cost of adding the black. Printing in two colours will cost you more (and printers think that black is a colour);

- Unless your house colour is pale, you could use a tint of it. A tint is effectively a diluted version, so a tint of black is grey, and a tint of red is pink. This is much cheaper than using a second colour (although it will cost you a little more than using only one). So for a cheap logo in two colours, you can use the house colour and a tint of it. Your printer will tell you that you can have any degree of dilution to create a range of tints, which are expressed in percentages: a 10 per cent tint is very pale, while a 90 per cent tint is almost as dark as the original colour. Two notes of caution about using tints, though. First, don't try using several different tints of the same colour on the page; it will look messy. Second, some beautiful colours have disgusting tints, so ask your printer to show you first what the tint will look like – a good printer will have a chart showing a range of tints;

- If you can't really afford a second colour for your logo but would like to use one, you can have a colour that you use only occasionally. So you exclude it from letters, invoices and so on, but when you print a smart brochure, or something with a slightly larger budget, you add in the second colour;

- You can introduce another colour in the paper that you print on. But bear in mind that in order to be consistent you need to choose a colour that you can easily reproduce on exhibition panels, signboards, glossy brochures and so on. So don't pick an obscure colour that is only produced by one paper manufacturer, and they don't do a glossy version, or one thick enough for folders or heavy brochures. Remember also that this colour is as much part of your corporate identity as the ink you print on it, so choose it with as much care. It should always be a pale colour or it will be difficult to read what you have typed or printed on it.

Finally, a good printer should be able to advise you on ways to keep the cost down. There are a lot of good printers around but there are also a few out there who may take advantage if they realise your inexperience, so choose a printer who has been recommended to you. Preferably visit a few and have a chat with them. A good printer will be one of your most valuable suppliers, so it's worth putting quite a bit of time and thought into choosing them.

Did it work?

There are lots of expensive ways to make sure you're getting the message across; we don't want to know about them, because we can't afford them. If ever you can afford them, I'll just tell you that they are all based on market research practices, and usually involve employing market research agencies. They can be very useful... but there's time enough to check that out once you've started buying books about 'Marketing Your Huge and Successful Business'.

For now, use a combination of common sense and experience. To apply the common sense, use the first rule of small business marketing: pretend you're a customer. Go through each of the aspects of your business that you listed in the previous exercise, and ask yourself, 'If I were a customer (or a potential customer), what message would this send to me?' And pester your friends some more – ask their opinions on your brochure design or your new system for dealing with complaints. Ask them in particular what sort of company they think your image projects.

As for the experience, see what happens. If you're projecting the right image, and projecting it clearly in everything you do, your business will reflect it. It takes time to build an image to the point where it sticks in everyone's mind, but you should be able to judge how you're doing from your customers' response.

Do people seem to remember your company name? Do you get a lot of word-of-mouth recommendations? Do customers make comments about your business? ('You're always so efficient', 'How nice to see a friendly face at the end of a hard week's work', 'Your reception area is looking very smart', 'It's not like you to be late with a delivery.') Most customers won't remark, but they are likely to be thinking the same thing as the customers who do. The important thing is that any comments you *do* get should be positive. If your customers are saying 'Come on! I've been through this with you twice already' or 'Cheer up!', you know you need to work a little harder on your image.

If you are doing any market research, of the type we looked at in Chapter 2, you could include questions about your image. But remember, people's impression of you is often unconscious so you'll have to think carefully about how to word the questions. Try something along the lines of 'If you had to describe The Office Plant Company in one word, which word would you choose?'

Assessing the success of your company's image is not an exact science, but you can be quite sure that you will maximise its positive impact if you:

- choose an image that suits you, your product or service, and your customers
- make sure you are consistent
- project a clear image and never contradict yourself
- make sure that all your actions are in line with the image you are trying to project.

4

PUBLIC RELATIONS

What is PR?

We've all heard of public relations, or PR, and we've got a vague idea of what it's all about. But what *exactly* does it mean? And do small companies really have to do it?

There are plenty of wordy and unintelligible definitions of PR, but essentially it is about consciously projecting the company image that we looked at in Chapter 3. We've already established that you send out messages to the public – your customers, potential customers, future employees, local community and so on – whether you like it or not. And Chapter 3 dealt with controlling the subliminal messages we give. This chapter is about how to strengthen your image further by putting across the message consciously and deliberately.

What's the point of PR?

PR doesn't sell products directly, but it's still more than worthwhile. Among the benefits of a strong, positive image are:

- people are more likely to buy your product or service if they like your company.
- people will be more likely to recommend you to others

- your name and product are more likely to be remembered
- you will find it easier to attract and retain good staff
- suppliers will be even more keen to get your business

A well run company can function without PR, but it will never function as well. And it will be an easy prey to any threat to its image, such as a news story that casts it in a bad light, or a competitor with a strong positive image. But one of the best reasons of all for using PR is that it's virtually free. That's got to be good news for a small business.

How do you do PR?

So what does PR actually involve? Well, you want to publicise your company and your products or services in a good light as often as possible. There are two kinds of image that you want to publicise:

1 A general, feel-good impression of the business; that it's friendly, successful, good to work for, and so on;
2 The specific aspects of the business that you have chosen as your key image points: that it's friendly, efficient and smart.

And there are, broadly speaking, three ways in which you can get this image across:

- in the papers
- on the radio and television
- through other routes (known as non-media PR)

In this chapter, we're going to look at each of these three in turn, and focus on how to get the best out of each.

—— Getting into the papers ——

This is probably the easiest type of PR. Once you're in the habit of it, you'll find you can get yourself regular newspaper coverage. It's not so easy to get into the national press unless you have a particularly good or unusual story, but you should be able to get your company name into the local (and regional) papers at least once a month (and free of charge). For most small businesses, the local press is the place to be. If your customers are local, and your staff are local, and maybe your suppliers too, you obviously want to concentrate your PR in the same place.

Cultivating contacts

The first thing you'll need to do is to find out who the local and regional press are. Presumably you know or even take some of the papers yourself. You'll find a listing in *BRAD*, which I mentioned in Chapter 2, at your local library. But really, the best thing is to get a copy of each of the papers. You'll find their contact details somewhere in their pages so you can draw up a list of them.

It's always a good idea to become acquainted with your local press. You'll get a picture of the kind of stories they like to include. And there's another reason for having a copy of the papers rather than just looking up their addresses in a directory. When you look through them, you'll also be able to check whether they have a special business page; many of the larger papers do.

The next job is to put names to the addresses – individual editors' names. You may well have to phone the switchboard to ask for the right name to use. As a general rule, if there's a business page you'll need to ask for the name of the business editor. Otherwise you'll want the name of the news editor. Add these names to your addresses and you can put together a press release mailing list. There are three other pieces of information you need to keep a note of:

1 The phone number of the paper, because you will need to telephone the press sometimes, as we'll see later;
2 The day the paper comes out, and its copy deadline. For the local weekly press, this is usually about two days before the paper comes out. So if it hits the news stands on Thursday, you probably have to submit your press releases by Tuesday morning at the latest (and they are more likely to be included if they turned up in plenty of time; say on Monday morning);
3 The name of the features editor. Most of the press releases you send out will be news items, and will therefore go to the news editor. But occasionally you may want the paper to run a feature article about your company, in which case you'll want to contact the features editor.

It's worth clarifying the difference between news and features. News is about a current story – you've just won a huge export order, for example. A feature is an article about a long term, ongoing subject, such as the growth in the number of people taking holidays abroad. If you're a high street travel agent you can encourage the local paper to run a feature on this, based around interviews with you and examples taken from your business. As a rule of thumb, if the story needs to be printed soon or it will go out of date, it's a news story. If it can wait – perhaps for several weeks – it's a feature article.

Getting to know the press

Now here's the thing that many small businesses never find out about the local press: they need you. Unlike the national papers, the locals operate on a minimum number of staff. They don't have the resources to go around dredging up news stories. They rely on the news coming to them. All you have to do is give them a good story, write the press release well enough that they don't have to spend time rewriting it, and they'll be delighted. As far as they are concerned, that's one less column to fill in the next issue.

There was a tiny catch in that last bit... 'all you have to do is give them a good story...'. How are you supposed to know what that is? We're about to run through some of the ground rules for a good story, but every paper will have its own angle – particular types of stories it's looking for, and so on. And the way to find out what is each editor's idea of a good story, is to ask them. So once you've found out who the key editors at your local papers are, you need to talk to them and, if possible, meet them.

First of all, ring them. Introduce yourself. Tell them (briefly) what your company is called and what it does. Explain that you'd like to be able to give them the kind of stories they are looking for, and it would be very helpful if you could meet for a chat so that they can tell you what kind of stories tend to interest them. Some will agree readily, others will be too busy to meet but should be happy to chat for a few minutes on the phone. Either way, you need to make sure they don't forget who you are five minutes later (they really are very busy people). The way to do this is to send them what's known as a press pack. It's a folder of useful pieces of background information about your company. You should always have a few press packs prepared, because they can be helpful if a news story breaks suddenly (one of your staff is injured in a machine accident, or you win the regional 'Best Small Business' award). The press pack will contain three quarters of what the press want to know without them having to ask you. It should include:

- your most recent press release;
- a fact sheet about your business – a brief history, product/service list, number of staff, latest figures, contact details, and so on;
- biographical notes on you and any other directors or partners;
- a 'backgrounder' – this is a press release that is along the lines of a feature article rather than a news story. It shouldn't go out of date too quickly and should be about industry trends, or your company's novel approach to dealing with the latest changes in the industry, or something along those lines;
- photographs – of you and your fellow partners or directors, and of your product or factory or some general but relevant illustration. If you sell a service and not a product you should be able to find a suitable photograph; for example, a travel agent could have a photograph of people sunbathing on the beach (we'll go on to see what makes a good photograph later in this chapter);
- your current sales literature.

Once you have made contact, start sending in the press releases. No paper will include a piece about your company every day, but the more you send, the more will get printed. You'll start to see what the saturation point for each paper is, and you can adjust the number you send accordingly. If the stories are good enough, though, it's quite possible to get a mention in the same paper three or four weeks in a row.

If one of the papers doesn't print any of your stories for a while, call the news editor – you know them all now, after all – and ask the reason. It may be very simple to make an adjustment that will get your stories printed. The other time to call the editors is if you have a particularly big story. Give them a ring and ask them to look out for it. Then ring them once it has arrived and ask if they need any more information. If you do this too often, it will obviously lose its impact. But do it once or twice a year – when the story is genuinely a particularly good one – and this should help to get it printed.

The trade press

You may well need to create another press list for the trade press. You know who your target customers are – if they read the trade press you need to cultivate these contacts too, in the same way as the local press. They will want slightly different stories – or the same story but with a different slant – from those that the local press want, and talking to them is the best way to find out what kind of item will interest them. According to some research, 40 per cent of buying decisions in large companies are made on the basis of information gathered from the trade press. So if you're selling to big businesses, you can't afford not to cultivate your trade press contacts.

What makes a good story?

As I've already said, the news editors themselves are the best people to tell you what kind of stories they want to print. But there are some general rules that apply to every story, no matter what paper you're sending it to.

- Imagine you are the news editor. What kind of story would you want to print? The local press want to print plenty of good news, for a start. And they want news with a local angle – because they know that's what their readers want. So anything to do with staff, job opportunities, local customers, local events and so on will catch their attention. The trade press are more interested in stories about business successes, new products and so on. They can vary a lot, however, so talk to them about it;
- Make sure the story is really as interesting to the reader as it is to you. It may be your bread and butter, but that doesn't automatically make it interesting to an outsider. You can practise the first rule of marketing here – pretend you're a customer. In this case, pretend you're a customer who is reading the local paper. If you knew nothing about this company, would you bother to read this story?
- Be truthful. If you twist the truth, or misrepresent it, you are likely to get found out. And that's an even better story for the press. Suppose you claim you're creating five new jobs by opening a new shop. That sounds great, and the local press will most likely print it. But if you're simultaneously laying off six people in the factory, because you're buying in more finished stock rather than making it yourself, you could wind up looking far worse than if you'd never said anything in the first place. It's never worth trying to get away with this kind of thing, because if you do get caught it can take literally years for people to forget the bad publicity about you. And you're quite likely to get caught; the six people you laid off will be on to the paper as soon as they read your story.

There should never be any shortage of material to make a good story about, once you get used to recognising it. Here is a list of the kind of ingredients that make for a good story:

- Topicality – anything of immediate relevance goes down well, such as the fifth anniversary of the business, or an announcement that you're taking on new staff. Just a word about announcements, here. A press release is, in itself, an announcement. You don't have to organise special events at which you publicise these pieces of good news, and then write a press release about it afterwards. You simply put out a press release in which you say 'Globetrotters Travel have announced that...'
- Good news – new jobs, sponsoring the local school, business expansion and so on;
- Human interest – a story that focuses on a local personality (not necessarily well-known): a member of staff whose suggestion has brought in £5000 of new business, for example;
- The unusual – anything wacky is popular with editors. For example, a customer who managed to persuade their cat down after two days stuck up a tree by luring it to safety with smoked salmon bought from your delicatessen;
- Humour – this is hard to create, because it can seem forced. But if the humour is genuinely there in the situation, play on it;
- Celebrities – if you can get a celebrity to use your product, open your new factory or attend your latest event, you've got a story;
- Children or animals – this plays on the sympathy angle, of course – and the press are suckers for it. These stories are always better for a good photo;
- Anything with a really good photo to illustrate it (we'll come to that a little later on).

Generating your own stories

If you really can't think of a good story about your business just now, make one up. Yes, I know I said you must always be truthful. You will be. You just invent the story first and then make it come true. There's a great benefit in this, in that you can create a story that casts you in exactly the light you want it to.

Suppose one of the key image words for your high street travel agency is 'helpful'. You want people to realise that you'll put yourself out, be flexible and if necessary stretch the rules for them (though never break them, of course). Perhaps you're worried that this aspect of your image isn't coming across as strongly as it might. This is a good time to generate a positive news story that shows how you've managed to help someone by giving better service than they could ever have expected.

Travel agents have access to low cost holidays; if you wait for cancellations or last minute bookings you can find a holiday – perhaps just a weekend break – for almost nothing. Now you just have to find someone worthy to give it to. Maybe someone has just been featured in the local paper who has had a run of bad luck. Maybe you know of someone who has lost out on a holiday because the travel company went bankrupt, or their house went up in flames the day before they were due to leave. Maybe you can get tickets to Disneyland for a local child who is recovering from a serious illness. This may seem callous and cynical when you read it in black and white. It's not. You are genuinely helping someone who needs it. There's no law that says you can't help people if it also benefits you.

EXERCISE

Now it's your turn to do some thinking. See if you can come up with three ideas for press releases about your business that you could write today. They don't have to be earth-shattering, front page headlines. Just stories that the local press would want to include somewhere in their papers. Don't try to write the whole press release (we haven't done that bit yet); just note down the idea.

Press release 1

Press release 2

Press release 3

In case you found this exercise difficult, and most of us find it harder until we get into the habit of it, I'll run through the ingredients I listed earlier and give you a suggestion or two for each. (You'll notice that several of the suggestions combine two or more ingredients.) They may not apply to your business, but they should spark off a few ideas.

- Topicality: new products or services. The fact that you now offer three different levels of travel insurance may not be riveting news, but the fact that you've just started offering holidays to Madagascar is certainly newsworthy;
- Good news: a big contract that secures jobs for at least two years perhaps. Or, from a different angle, a customer who has had success using your product. Perhaps you produce animal feeds; you could put together a story about a prize bull that has just won 'best of breed' at the agricultural show after being fed on your brand;
- Human interest: one of your staff is being made a director or partner, or has won a travel agents' association 'Employee of the Year' award;
- The unusual: a customer has asked you to arrange a travelling holiday for them that visits fourteen countries around the world in as many days – and you've managed to do it;
- Humour: how about the cat stuck up the tree story again? Or perhaps

you've run a competition among your customers offering a discount to whoever can come up with the oddest travel experience, and now you're announcing the winning entries;

- Celebrities: celebrities are always being asked to do things, and they have to say no much of the time (though for a large event, especially if you're prepared to pay, it's always worth asking – several months in advance). But minor celebrities, only well known at the local level, are good enough for you. And local politicians and councillors will often agree to attend events – they want to be associated with successful local enterprise. So invite the local MP to open your new factory, or ask a local actor to present your sponsorship cheque to the local children's home;

- Children or animals: perhaps you've just invited the local school to bring a group of children to look round your factory. Or maybe you have donated your obsolete 486 computer to the local animal sanctuary;

- Anything with a really good photo to illustrate it: the sponsored staff parachute jump in aid of a local charity, for example. (This is also a good example of a story you could have generated yourself, especially if you wanted your company to appear innovative and adventurous.)

If ever you get stuck for a story in future it's a good idea to look through the first part of this chapter again and then repeat the exercise above.

Writing a press release

This is easy, as long as you follow a couple of simple guidelines: don't try to be clever, and remember to start with the punchline (this goes against the grain with any natural raconteurs). This is easiest to illustrate by following the life cycle of a press release.

Use a clear headline that tells the story

You need to understand how busy the editor is. Your press release will arrive on the desk along with dozens of others. The editor will scan them all quickly, reading just the headline to see what the story is about. Any release that doesn't instantly shout its message will be binned. So the headline must be clear, and must summarise the story. Make it as informative, positive and interesting as possible: don't say *Globetrotters' staff raise money with parachute jump* when you could say *Travel staff parachute to help local children's ward*. One more thing about headlines: any editor who uses the story will rewrite the headline. They don't want to risk duplicating the same headline as the other local press. So you are writing the headline only for the editor – not for the readers.

Flesh out the details in the next paragraph

If your press release has been shortlisted (in other words, it hasn't been binned yet), the editor will read the first paragraph. By the end of the first paragraph, its fate will have been virtually decided. Give the editor all the salient facts in a brief introduction (two sentences at the most). If you didn't get your name into the headline, make sure it is in the first paragraph. *Staff from the local travel agency Globetrotters took to the skies themselves to raise funds for the local children's ward. Their sponsored parachute jump from 5,000 feet raised £1,500 for the Gibson ward, which is threatened with closure.* You'll notice that the release is written in the third person, as though it were being written by the editor (who of course doesn't really have time to write any articles).

Give the rest of the information – most important bits first

If you've made it this far past the editor – well done. With a bit of practice, all your releases should get this far. The only thing now deciding whether your story makes it into the paper or not, is the competition. If the editor has been flooded with good stories, and there's plenty of news around, you still have to fight a little harder to be sure that yours is included. What the editor wants is a clear story, well written and well presented. That way it will take precedence over the badly presented press releases that can't be used unless they are rewritten first. So here are the key rules for writing the body of the press release:

- Report the story objectively. If it reads like an ad, the editor will throw it out. So no glowing descriptions of your products or your business. Let the story speak for itself;
- The information you give should answer the questions: *who* (did it), *what* (did they do), *when* (did they do it), *why* (did they), *where* (did it happen) and *how* (did it happen);
- Keep your language simple and your sentences short;
- If there isn't room to include the whole article, the editor will cut it

PRESS RELEASE
TRAVEL STAFF PARACHUTE TO HELP LOCAL CHILDREN'S WARD

For immediate release

Staff from the local travel agency Globetrotters took to the skies themselves to raise funds for the local children's ward. Their sponsored parachute jump from 5000 feet raised £1500 for the local hospital's Gibson ward, which is threatened with closure.

Last Friday, four of Globetrotters' staff took the afternoon off work to jump out of an aeroplane over the Wiltshire downs. After two hours of intensive training the four, none of whom had ever tried parachuting before, were taken up to 5000 feet in the plane to make the jump.

Globetrotters were raising money to help save the Gibson ward, which has twenty beds for children suffering from serious illnesses. The ward has been told that it may have to close next year unless more money can be found to keep it open. A campaign was launched in March to raise funds to save it.

Managing director Pat Keen, one of the four who did the jump, said: 'We wanted to do our bit to help keep the ward open, and this seemed like a good idea at the time. We had second thoughts just before we jumped, but it was exhilarating and we really enjoyed it, especially because we knew we were doing it for a good cause'.

PRESS RELEASE ENDS

28 April 1996

For further information contact Pat Keen at Globetrotters from Mon–Fri between 9:00 a.m. and 5:30 p.m. on (01234) 567890, or evenings and weekends on (01234) 098765.

from the bottom up. So the further up the page a piece of information is, the more likely it is to be used. So say the important things first;

- Try to avoid using long titles or names of organisations, especially near the beginning of the story, as they put people off reading. If you have to use them (and you do sometimes), keep them to a minimum, and use abbreviations or initials after the first mention;
- Use quotes. These add human interest, but should go near the end of the story. Quote one of the staff, or the hospital. The easiest way to do this is to write the quote you want to use yourself, and then ask the person you're 'quoting', 'Do you mind if I quote you as saying this?'

Present the press release clearly

There is a simple standard format for laying out press releases. It's important that you follow it because it makes life easier for the editor – which means your story is more likely to get printed:

- Print the press release on A4 paper, headed PRESS RELEASE and with your logo on it. Letterheads will do fine, though businesses that can afford it often have paper specially prepared (much like a letterhead without the address and legal details). This is barely more expensive (it saves on letterheads, after all); you may want to talk to your printer about it;
- Under the words PRESS RELEASE, print the release date. This is the date when the information becomes public. If you want the press to print it straight away, you can put 'For immediate release'. If you don't want them to print the story until after the parachute jump has happened, you should put 'Embargoed until...' and then give the time and date after which they can use the story;
- Use double spacing, and print on only one side of the paper. If you get to the bottom of the page, don't print on the reverse but start a fresh sheet and staple the two together (so the editor can't inadvertently separate them);
- Don't exceed 250 words. Ideally, try to stick to one sheet of paper only. Editors like this – it gives them less to read – and they can always ask you for more information if they think the story warrants it;
- At the end of the press release, type PRESS RELEASE ENDS. The editor knows that any information that appears after this is not intended for publication;

- After PRESS RELEASE ENDS print the date (today's date, not the release date). Then give contact details for any further information, including an evening/weekend phone number if possible.

Getting the best from photographs

A press release is more likely to be printed if it is accompanied by a good photograph. In fact, if the photo is good enough, it will get used even if the story is pretty weak. Here are a few practical points to bear in mind:

- Your article is several times more likely to be read if it has a good photo printed alongside it;
- The press will send out their own photographer only for a big story. Generally you will have to provide your own photos;
- The local press are likely to want black and white photographs. The trade press may want colour or black and white. Find out who wants what, and organise the photo session accordingly. Colour photos will often not reproduce in black and white, especially in newspaper quality, and the press will often drop them rather than attempt it. Newspapers and magazines that print in colour will probably want transparencies rather than prints;
- If you can't afford all these photos (and this can be a problem for small businesses), ration yourself to sending them out only with stories that really need them, or when there's an opportunity for a particularly good picture, or just send them to the key papers, not all of them. You can mention, after the end of the press release, that photos are available on request. That way you only have to send them out to people who are actually going to use them;
- If you can't afford a professional photographer (which is quite likely) – or at least not all the time – find a really good amateur. It's important to use well taken photos. You may be able to do this yourself, but if you're in any doubt apply rule five of small business marketing – know your limitations. One of your staff might turn out to be a good photographer, or a friend's teenage son or daughter who will take photos for you for a fraction of the cost of a professional photographer;
- Save any good photos, especially of key staff, products or premises, in case you want to use them again later;
- On the back of every photo you send, you should glue a piece of paper with a caption that explains the picture fully, and gives your

company name so that if the photo becomes separated from the press release the editor can reunite them without too much difficulty.

That's all the technical stuff. Now let's get arty. A good photo is more likely to be printed than an average or poor one. So what makes a good photo? Here are a few clues:

- action or movement
- an unusual subject, activity or angle
- people involved in what they are doing rather than looking at the camera
- people using a product rather than standing next to it or holding it

The worst photos – and local papers are full of them – are mugshots of people grinning inanely at the camera while someone else, also grinning inanely, hands them a cheque. This is the competition you face in the local press, and it's not hard to beat. If you can't get a shot of your staff jumping out of the parachute, don't settle for one of you handing a cheque to the hospital manager, while grinning inanely. How about one of the children on the ward watching a parachuting doll being demonstrated by one of your staff?

— Getting on to radio and television —

This isn't so different from getting into the papers. You should go about it in exactly the same way: put the local radio and television stations on to your press list and send your press releases to them. Find out who the editors of the local news programmes are, phone them, ask what kind of stories they are interested in and so on.

Of course, you won't get on to the airwaves as often as you get into the press. The local weekly paper runs hundreds of stories; the local news programmes run only a few. But the principles are still exactly the same. What bothers most people is what to do on those special occasions when you get a phone call saying 'We got your press release. It's an interesting story. Can we come and interview you?' (Or 'Can you come to the studio to do an interview?')

Handling interviews

I'm not going to talk about handling interviews where the interviewer wants to catch you out – that's a different exercise altogether and it's strictly the damage limitation branch of PR. If it's on the cards, buy a book specialising in the subject – it will be a good investment. However, it rarely happens in well run small businesses, so we'll concentrate on the times when the media pick up on your press release and want to publicise it for you, and for the interest of their viewers and listeners.

However short you already think media interviews are, it will be even shorter when you get there. So decide in advance what you're going to say, and make it brief. Three key points to get across at the most: we're a travel agency, we wanted to help the local children's ward, so we did a sponsored parachute jump. Those are the things you want everyone to know – that's why you did the jump and sent the press release in the first place. Whatever the interviewer asks you, just make sure those three points come across. They won't be trying to thwart you, but they may think their listeners are more interested in what it feels like to jump from a plane at 5000 feet than in the fact that you're a travel agent. That's probably true, but this is a deal. You gave them the story after all. You can tell them everything they want to know about jumping out of planes – in exchange for them allowing you to mention that you're a travel agent.

Practise your interview in advance. You should be able to work out roughly what they're going to ask you ('how does it feel to jump out of a plane?'). Get a colleague or one of those long-suffering friends of yours to pretend to be the interviewer, and rehearse your answers. For example: 'Well, you'd have thought that, being a travel agent, I'd be very used to planes. And normally I am. But I really wasn't prepared for the feeling...' and so on. Practising improves your performance on the day, and it helps to ease nerves.

There are a few more practical points to make about doing interviews:

- If you're going to the studio, make sure you arrive in plenty of time – especially if it's a live interview;
- Don't have a drink beforehand, no matter how nervous you are – especially if you're very nervous in fact;
- If you need to go to the lavatory just before the interview, that's fine. In fact, it's normal. For goodness sake say so; the interviewer won't mind at all;

- If you're sitting for the interview, sit straight. If you sit on the edge of your chair you'll find it much harder to slouch;
- If you're prone to gabble, try to slow your speech down a little;
- For television interviews, choose your clothes to match your company image. If it's friendly, efficient and smart, for example, stick to standard smart clothes but keep it friendly with a bright colour or cheerful accessories. Make sure the clothes you choose are comfortable. Resist at all costs the temptation to wear those new shoes you haven't broken in yet, or the shirt with the overstarched collar. You can do without those sorts of distractions;
- Use a mirror to check your teeth, hair, tie, earrings, flies or anything else obvious before you go on on television.

Radio and television interviews can seem overawing, but they are really just conversations like any other if you can learn to ignore all the equipment around you. It's not so scary once you get stuck into it. You will probably enjoy it and you may even develop quite a taste for it. The most important thing is to concentrate on the interviewer, and simply be yourself.

EXERCISE

Here's a nice, easy, relaxing exercise for you to do. Watch your local news programme every night for a week (video it if you don't get back from work in time for it). Pick out all the interviews with people similar to you, who aren't used to being on television. They may be business people or they may be schoolteachers, or community leaders, or chairs of residents' associations. Consider the following points:

1 What is your first impression of them?
2 Are they answering the questions?
3 Do you think they are getting *their* message across?
4 What do you think is their best skill as an interviewee?
5 What do you think is their weakest point as an interviewee?

You should find that once you get into the habit of watching other people being interviewed you learn a great deal from it. The following week, listen to the local radio for half an hour a day – maybe in the car – and repeat the exercise.

Non-media PR

There is a whole category of PR we haven't looked at yet, which doesn't involve the press, radio or television at all: non-media PR. You won't necessarily want to practise all the various PR opportunities that you'll find listed below – some of them may not suit your business in any case – but you may well find that one or two of them could work very well for you.

Events

This covers all events that aren't put on for the benefit of the press. For example, you could throw a party to launch your next big new product, and invite all your top customers, prospects and suppliers along. Or hold an open day to invite them on a factory tour. Give them a glass of wine and a buffet, and an information pack. If you can, give them a free gift as well.

Your reputation among the locals may be important to you. Perhaps that's where you recruit many of your staff, or perhaps they don't like your lorries trundling past their houses and you want to compensate them for putting up with it. You could throw a Christmas party for all the local kids each year, or run sponsored events to raise money for a local cause.

Sponsorship

Small businesses tend to assume that they can't afford to give sponsorship, without even thinking about it. But you almost certainly can afford it. The point is that it's the thought that matters, not the value. And you may well be able to donate goods in kind, rather than having to give cash. There are three guidelines here:

- Try not to give to the same cause as everyone else; no one will notice you among many. You may get a nice warm glow from doing it – and please go ahead and do it if that's the aim – but as a PR exercise, it's worth almost nothing;
- If it's at all possible, try to find a cause that has a connection with your business, because it will help people to remember you. For example, a florist could donate used window boxes that are still in reasonable condition to the local retirement home;

- Make sure people know you've done it. Ask for your name to be printed on the programme of the school play that you donated props for, or get a press release in the paper. But make your sponsorship public, or it isn't part of *public* relations.

Giving talks

Contact local organisations and offer to talk to their members about something you're an authority on, through your work. Talk about how to have a safe, trouble-free holiday (making sure that Globetrotters is mentioned on the advance programme as well as your name). Or invite yourself along to the local school to talk about careers in the travel industry.

Newsletters

You could start up a newsletter to send to your customers and prospects. This works particularly well if you have a healthy sized mailing list and a broad range of products, and works especially well in the business-to-business sector. A few pointers:

- Make yourself bring it out regularly, and on time. It looks sloppy and inefficient if you don't. It doesn't have to be long, and it doesn't have to come out more than three times a year (this is the minimum that really works, otherwise your customers have time to forget about it completely in between issues);
- As far as print quality and so on is concerned, follow the guidelines for image that we looked at in Chapter 3. You can still look smart on a budget;
- Unsubtle advertising isn't popular with newsletter readers. Follow the same rule as you do for press releases – let the articles speak for themselves;
- Include news articles about your business, by all means, but remember what the reader is after: something that they can benefit from. So tell them what new products you're launching (and what they can do for them), show ways of using your current products or services in ways they hadn't thought of, let them know about any discounts or offers you're running, and so on;
- Include interviews with customers (if they're happy with your products they'll probably agree willingly), and customer case histories, as this helps the reader to relate to the story, and adds credibility;

- Mail your newsletter to your suppliers as well – it can only help to build a stronger relationship with them.

Did it work?

It's very easy to tell whether your PR is working, although it's difficult to measure it precisely. That's OK; rule four of small business marketing is don't try to be too perfect. It's difficult to quantify which of the local papers are most worth getting into, and whether four paragraphs on page 5 of this paper is better than six paragraphs on page 11 of that one. (Big businesses have nothing better to do than worry over this kind of question.) As far as you're concerned, if you're in the papers more than you used to be, it's working.

The press

Cut out all the press articles that follow your press releases, and keep a special file for them or stick them in a scrapbook. Keep your original press release with them. Check how much of this press release the editors chose to rewrite. They tend to rewrite the first paragraph for the same reasons they change the headline, but after that they'll leave your version alone if they like it (bar cutting it if it's too long). If they make changes, note what they are and see if you can work out why they weren't so happy with your wording; this is one of the best ways to improve your writing style. And think about which press releases they printed and which they didn't – occasionally stories are excluded simply because there's so much other news that week, but after a while you should start to see a pattern of which types of press releases are more popular.

Note down the date that each article appeared, in which paper, and who else you sent it to. Again, you should start to see who is most likely to print your stories (and photos), and how often they run one of your press releases.

Radio and television

Record radio and television appearances if you can, and listen to yourself critically. Ask your friends and colleagues for their honest opinion (you have to be forgiving to run a small business successfully). See how many people that you meet say 'I heard you on the radio.' It's hard to gauge the effectiveness of radio and television appearances very accurately, but you'll get a feel for the effect it's having.

Non-media PR

You'll get a fair idea of the impression that local sponsorship is making, but it's a long slow build-up. However as long as the public knows about it, it is bound to be beneficial. Events and talks are easier – you'll be able to see whether the people who attended start to make new enquiries about products, or increase their orders from you. Again, these events are not selling operations, but you'll notice over time.

A crucial factor in measuring PR is a rule that is usually quoted in relation to advertising (it actually goes for both): whenever you speak to a new lead or enquiry, ask them where they heard of you. And I mean *every* time. If you forget, call them back and ask – they won't mind. If you don't, you could be wasting your efforts on something that doesn't work. Perhaps none of them knows about your local sponsorship, but several of them attended talks that you gave.

If you run any customer questionnaires of the type that we looked at in Chapter 2, you can ask their opinion of the newsletter. You'll also get a fair idea of their views by whether they respond. Just because you're not hard selling or advertising in it, doesn't mean they won't call you and say 'I hadn't realised you offer discounts to businesses that book more than twenty flights a year through Globetrotters. Can you tell me more about it?'

It's actually quite easy to judge whether your PR efforts are working, and which are working best. And after a while, you'll start to realise what a wonderfully cheap form of publicity good PR can be.

5

CUSTOMER CARE

Depending on the nature of your business, it will cost you between three and seven times more to recruit new customers than it costs to hang on to those you've already got. Finding new customers can involve advertising, buying in mailing lists, printing more brochures, costly time spent persuading them to buy from you, and many more expenses. Of course you have to keep doing this, or your customer base will slowly dwindle as your existing customers move away, go bankrupt, die or whatever else.

Nevertheless, you should give priority to persuading your existing customers to stay with you; it's a far more cost-effective way of doing business. To do this, you need to make sure that they enjoy doing business with you. You want them to come off the phone, or leave your shop or office, thinking 'What nice people' or 'That was easy' or 'How efficient they are'. These feelings are completely different from their attitudes to your product or service (which you will make sure are equally positive, of course). These are emotional responses to you, your staff (if you have any) and your business, and they are an integral part of your company image.

What is customer care?

Customer care is the term given to all the techniques and practices which cultivate this positive emotional attitude from your customers. These techniques are not one aspect of your business. They constitute an approach which you should apply every time you deal with a customer, by post, on the phone or face to face; whether you are handling an enquiry, taking an order or making a delivery. Customer care is all about quality. In fact, the only definition of 'quality' that all the experts seem to agree on is 'quality is what the customer wants.'

We have already looked at several of the broader aspects of customer care in Chapter 3. In this chapter we'll look at some of the more specific applications:

- the personal touch
- efficiency
- being flexible
- telephone techniques
- coping with complaints.

These techniques together will help you to improve the loyalty of your customers, so that next time one of your competitors drops their prices or runs a big advertising campaign, your customers will be less tempted to switch to them.

The personal touch

Customer care is about human nature: we all want to be liked, valued, appreciated and looked after. So show your customers that you feel this way about them. The first step is to treat them as an individual, and not just another customer. You want them to feel that you'll notice if they stop buying from you. So make them feel liked and cared for by being friendly and giving personal service. These skills are absolutely crucial for everyone who ever has to speak to a customer, so if you have staff, train them all in these techniques.

Be friendly

This should be the simplest, most obvious thing in the world. But how often have you been greeted – face to face or over the phone – by someone blank and impersonal, or even surly and unwelcoming? People respond to the behaviour they meet with: if you are friendly, your customers will instinctively be friendly in return. And won't that make your life easier, as well as making your business more profitable? Here are the top ten rules to follow in order to present a friendly image:

1 Smile – every time you greet a customer;
2 Never ignore a customer, even if you can't deal with them straight away. Acknowledge them the moment you see them, smile, and say 'I'll be with you as soon as I can';
3 Try not to keep people waiting but if you have to, always apologise for it;
4 Never keep a customer waiting while you finish a private conversation;
5 If you can't help a customer, go and find someone who can;
6 Give your customer your full attention all the time. Don't sort paperwork, look for something you've lost, write notes (except about your conversation with them) or anything else while you're with them. Never eat in front of them. And if the phone rings while you're with a customer, leave it. (If this happens frequently you should arrange for someone else to answer the phone, or at least get an answerphone.)
7 If you need information, ask for it. But do it politely: not 'Give me you name' but 'Would you mind giving me your name?'
8 Always let the customer know what you're doing. For example, 'I'll just go and see if there's one in the stockroom; I'll be two or three minutes.'
9 Never criticise a customer, nor imply criticism by making comments such as 'You should have rung before 5:00 p.m. if you wanted to speak to sales.'
10 Never let it show if you disapprove of a customer's manner, clothes or anything else.

Be personal

This isn't as rude as it sounds. What I mean is, personalise your dealings with each of your customers:

1 Address your customers by name. If you don't know their name, ask them. Then use it; not to excess (which can be irritating) but at least use it at the beginning and end of the conversation;
2 Tell the customer your name. Unless your customers are very formal and old-fashioned, invite them to address you by your first name;

3 Look for something relevant to the customer to comment on, that is
personal to them rather than related to your business. Maybe you
like dogs and you've spotted one in the back of their car. You could
say: 'What a beautiful labrador; I've got a retriever myself. They're
lovely dogs.' Perhaps you like their jacket – why not ask them
where they got it? Or when they give you their address you could
say 'Edinburgh? That's a lovely city. I was there a couple of years
ago.' Just one proviso – don't keep customers chatting for hours.
You can't afford the time, and they probably can't either. To give
you an example: as I'm writing this, the chimney-sweep has just
left. He's friendly, efficient and reasonably priced, but he spends
half an hour sweeping the chimneys and an hour chatting if you let
him. Meanwhile, my computer is sitting waiting for me to get back
to it. I don't like to be rude, because he thinks he's being friendly,
but I've been known to change suppliers in the past simply because
they won't stop talking when I'm busy.

Give a little bit more

Finally, and importantly, always find a way to go a little bit further
than the customer expects. Suppose you sell flat-packed shelf units
for customers to assemble themselves. Put a note in with the instruc-
tions saying 'If you have problems assembling this shelf unit, please
give us a ring on this number and we'll do our best to help you'.

If you run a garage, you could leave a free anti-mist windscreen cloth in
every car when you complete its service. Globetrotters travel agency
could send all their customers a 'Don't forget to pack...' checklist to arrive
in the post a few days before their holiday starts, listing passports, trav-
eller's cheques, and so on. Or an estate agent could give customers a
checklist of 'things to do before you move...': insurance, gas, water, elec-
tricity, informing your bank, and so on. Some shops and suppliers keep a
supply of sweets to offer to their customer's children – at least you'll earn
the kids' loyalty, and they'll drag their parents back again and again.

Saying thank-you

You can also give your customers the occasional thank-you present. This
is different from a free gift because you make it clear (verbally, perhaps,
or in a covering letter) that it is a token of appreciation for their custom.
If you run The Office Plant Company, for example, you could give each

customer a free plant on the first anniversary of their signing a contract with you. And perhaps a more expensive plant on the fifth anniversary.

Well-planned thank-you gifts will more than earn their keep in improved customer loyalty; if repeat business is important to you, you should be doing it. If you're going to give your customers thank-you presents of any kind, make sure the value of the present matches the value of the customer. Employ rule one of small business marketing: pretend you're a customer. If you spent £1500 buying shelf units and bedside tables from a furniture company, how would you feel if they offered you a voucher giving you £2 off your next purchase? Possibly a little offended. It would be more appropriate to offer them, say, a coffee table that retails at £30 (and costs you only £15). If you can't afford that, it's better to offer them nothing than to insult them by suggesting that their custom is of low value.

If you really feel you can't afford thank-you gifts for your customers (even after you've calculated the value of the increased loyalty it will generate), consider giving fewer gifts. So The Office Plant Company could skip the first anniversary present but still give the fifth anniversary gift - or at least the tenth. Or show that you remember them without an actual gift - give your best customers priority ordering (and let them know it), or send them Christmas cards, or invite them for an annual 'thanks for your custom' drink if they are local.

EXERCISE

Doing something extra

There's always something extra you can do for your customers. Note down in the space below three extras you could offer your customers that they aren't expecting.

Thank-you presents

If you sell to customers who buy from you more than once, and whose loyalty you want to cultivate, write down three ideas for presents you could give the most loyal of them to say thank-you – your custom is appreciated.

Efficiency

It's no good just being friendly and pleasant, important though that is. You must also give the customers what they want with the least hassle for them. That means making it simple and making it quick. Here are the most important points to remember:

1 Make your order forms, and anything else you ask the customer to fill in, as easy as possible to follow. When you design the forms, get a few friends who don't know your system to test it for you and tell you if it's as simple as you think it is;

2 Deal with enquiries promptly. If someone asks for a copy of your catalogue, get it in the post tonight, not in two or three days' time;

3 Don't use jargon unless you're sure the customer is familiar with it;

4 If you're taking down messages – over the phone or face to face – always repeat the message back to the customer to make sure you've got it right. This applies especially to numbers such as phone numbers and postcodes;

5 Always pass on messages or information promptly;

6 If you need the customer's file or computer details to sort out their enquiry effectively, go and get it – don't try to remember it. It's better to ask them to wait for a moment at the start than to fetch the file half way through the conversation and then make them repeat all the details they have just given you;

7 Repeat anything complicated or important to the customer to show that you've understood: 'And I've got to have it delivered before Saturday week.' 'Delivery before Saturday 11th. That's fine.'

8 Always finish dealing with one customer before you move on to the next. If you're still filling out the last customer's order form after he or she has left and another customer walks in, look up and smile, and say 'I'll be with you in just a moment'. If you don't, you run the risk of forgetting to complete the order form, or even forgetting it all together. If the new customer seems irritated you can always explain 'If I don't complete the last customer's order while it's still in my head, there's a danger I may forget something.' The new customer will realise that you'd do the same for him or her. (It should go without saying that if this happens frequently you should simplify your order-taking procedure, have someone else available to serve the next customer, or in some way improve the system.)

9 Keep your promises – and if you can, better them (this is part of giving the customer a little more, which we covered in the last section of this chapter). Always get back to customers if you tell them you will. And if you tell them you'll confirm the delivery date by the end of the week, confirm it on Thursday. Or even Wednesday.

10 Follow up – if somebody wanted delivery urgently by Friday, call on Friday to make sure it arrived.

Being flexible

Now here's an area where you have a huge advantage being a small company. You must have contacted large suppliers before and asked them to do something a little out of the ordinary for you – send the order and the invoice to different addresses, customise the product or service in some way, or process an order in less than the usual time (and you don't mind paying extra) – only to be told 'I'm sorry, we can't do that', or 'I'm afraid the system doesn't work like that', or 'The computer can't process it.'

You don't have to be bound by these unhelpful procedures, that are designed to make life easier for the company at the expense of the customer. You can give customers what they want. Forget the computer: if it can't cope, you can process the order manually and then feed doctored information into the computer afterwards so that it still generates an invoice. Of course, some things are not cost effective – but the customer will usually pay: 'Yes, we *can* deliver a flat-pack shelf unit to the Shetland Islands; we'd have to charge you the extra on the delivery costs but we can get it to you in seven days.' This example illustrates another point as well: if there is a piece of bad news to impart ('we'd have to charge you the extra'), make sure you finish up with a piece of good news ('we can get it to you in seven days').

Flexibility will put you ahead of your bigger competitors, and you'll really score with the customers. So make sure you offer that little extra that your competitors can't at every opportunity. If it costs you extra, pass the cost on to the customers if you need to. As long as you tell them in advance, they'll understand; at least they have the option. Your competitors would just have told them 'The computer can't process it'.

Telephone techniques

All of the guidelines we've just covered apply just as much, of course, when you're speaking to your customers over the phone: use the personal touch, be efficient and be friendly. However, there are some additional things to remember when you talk to customers on the phone, that don't apply when you're dealing with them face to face.

The personal touch

1 When you answer the phone, smile. You can hear it down the phone;
2 If you are answering an outside call, say 'Good morning' or 'Good afternoon', and then give your company name. If a call has been put through to you, say 'Good morning' or 'Good afternoon' and then give your own name. Either way, sound as if this is the first time you've answered the phone today; don't use a weary or sing-song tone that makes customers feel they are the fiftieth faceless voice you've had to deal with since breakfast. And 'good morning' acts as a tuning fork, so they're more likely to catch your name or the company name;
3 Concentrate on the call – just because they can't see you, it doesn't mean they won't know if you're trying to do something else at the same time;
4 Show that you're listening: make 'mmm' and 'uh-huh' noises, and repeat back key phrases;
5 Don't give people orders, such as 'Hold on'. Solicit their co-operation: 'Would you mind holding on?' And remember that they might mind. So give them a chance to say 'Actually, I am in a bit of a hurry. Do you think you could call me back with the answer?'

Be efficient

1 Every phone should have a pen and notepad by it. It should be a capital offence to remove these;
2 When the phone rings, answer it within three rings;
3 Always answer a ringing phone, even if it's not yours. At least you can take a message;

4 As soon as customers tell you who they are, write it down so you can call them by name;

5 At the end of the call, confirm what happens next: 'I'll put the brochures in the post to you today, and then I'll give you a ring towards the end of next week.'

6 If you tell someone you'll call them back, always do it within the time you've promised, even if it's only to say 'I said I'd call you at 3.00 to let you know what was happening. I still can't get in touch with the driver so there's no news, but I'll call again when I hear anything. In any case I'll ring you before we close at 5:30.'

7 Always repeat back messages, especially any numbers;

8 All phone messages should include the time of the call, the customer's name and number, and your name if there could be any doubt as to who took the message. Make it clear to the person receiving the message whether they are supposed to be making the next move;

9 Pass all messages on promptly;

10 Finish writing notes and messages before you answer the next call.

Coping with complaints

Even the best-run companies, with the highest quality products or services, get the occasional complaint. We're only human, and sooner or later all of us make the odd mistake, however hard we try. And some customers complain about things that turn out not to be our fault. So you need to know how to handle complaints when you do get them.

Inside the customer's mind

First of all, you need to think about the customer's feelings. Some people will be civil when they complain and others won't. To some extent this is determined by their personality, but their view of your company will also play a part. The more closely you follow the points we've covered so far in this chapter, the more friendly your customers will be towards you, and the less likely they are to be angry if they make a complaint.

But there will still be one or two who will contact you in an angry mood. You should handle them in exactly the same way that you handle the others – only more carefully. Which makes them a good example to help you focus on the way people feel when they complain – the angry ones are simply ordinary complainers who are pushed to extremes. And the easiest way to imagine how they feel is to remember your own experiences as a complainer.

EXERCISE

Think about the last time you were annoyed when you complained, and note down your responses to the following questions:

1 Why did you go to the lengths of complaining (rather than not register your complaint)?

2 What attitude did you expect to get from the person you contacted with your complaint?

3 What attitude did you want from them?

4 What attitude did you get?

5 What action did you want from them?

6 What action did you get?

7 How quickly was your complaint resolved?

8 Have you bought from the company since?

9 What two or three words would you use to describe the way your complaint was handled?

There are no right or wrong answers to these questions, of course, but there are certain feelings that most people share about making complaints; you may well find that you can identify with them. I'll go through the most important points before we examine how to deal with complaints, because you need to know how the customer feels before you can work out your own response to the complaint.

- Why complain? This may seem obvious – because there was something wrong. But in fact, research shows that for the average business only one in every twenty-five unhappy customers bothers to complain. Many of them simply don't come back, or need very little persuasion to switch to a competitor. What's more, they may tell up to twenty other people that they were dissatisfied with your company. On the other hand, if they complain and you deal with them well, they will almost certainly come back, often more loyal than before. So you *want* your unhappy customers to complain, and to go away thinking 'Everyone makes mistakes, but at least when this company makes a mistake I know they will put it right quickly and efficiently';

- What attitude do people expect when they complain? The answer to this helps to explain why many people don't complain. They often expect to be treated with irritation, frustration or even disbelief. This is why many complainers start out aggressively – after all, the best form of defence is attack. A complainer is usually nervous, worried they won't be taken seriously, and frightened that you'll make them feel small or stupid. *You* may know that you're going to treat them with sympathy and patience, but they don't;

- What attitude do people want? They want their concerns acknowledged. They want you to let them know that they are entitled to complain and that you sympathise with the problems they have suffered. This removes their fear of being made to feel silly, or not being taken seriously;

- What action do people want? If complainers are riled they will behave as small children (and most adults) do in this situation: they will become unreasonable and ask for the impossible. For example, 'I want you to send someone up this afternoon to assemble these shelves for me.' But if you don't rile people, they will be reasonable: 'Could you send me a ready-assembled shelf unit?' People complain because they want the problem resolved; once they know that you're trying to help, they'll be reasonable;

- How fast should you aim to resolve each complaint? Research indicates that the faster you respond, the more likely the customer is to be satisfied and to the complainant buy from you again. Even if you can't get the new shelf unit to the complainant in less than a week, the important thing is to let the customer know within minutes (or an hour or two at most) that you will be sending the unit to them and they can expect it next Wednesday. In fact, people are prepared to wait longer for the solution if they are kept informed regularly of what is happening;

- Will customers who complain buy from you again? The odds are that they will if you handle the complaint well, and they won't if you handle it badly. It helps if you respond quickly, and if the customer has contact your organisation only once. Every time they have to call back, the chances of them buying from you again are reduced.

The key rules for handling complaints

Now that we've established the customer's side of things, I'll summarise the main conclusions we can draw from this about how to handle complaints.

Encourage dissatisfied customers to complain

- Let people know that it's worth complaining if they are unhappy. Tell them by printing messages on delivery notes, instruction sheets or packaging. For example, 'We hope you will be very satisfied with this shelf unit. However, if you do experience any problems, please let us know...'
- Let them know how to complain - many dissatisfied customers simply don't know who to contact, or where, or how: '...please let us know by calling us on (01234) 567890 or writing to the Marketing Director at the address below.' Many people would rather phone, so make sure you give them the option;
- Most of all, show people that it's worth complaining by demonstrating, when they do have a complaint, that you will resolve the problem efficiently and helpfully.

Adopt the right attitude

- If it's humanly possible, make sure that anyone who answers the phone or stands behind the counter is capable of handling complaints, so they don't have to be passed on. (If you're in business on your own you're at an advantage here.)
- The first thing to do is to show that you're on the customers' side and you want to help; this will allay their fears. Start by listening

to them: they want to get the problem off their chest. Their problem is not directly that your shelf unit fell apart; it is that they have wasted their time assembling it, that they are frustrated, or that it made them late. This is what you must let them say. For a small complaint, it will take only a second. If the problem has had serious repercussions they may need to let off steam for a minute or two.

- While you are listening, acknowledge their feelings. This doesn't have to be more than a sympathetic smile or an 'Oh dear' down the phone. Or you could say 'how frustrating for you' or 'I can see how confusing that must have been.' If you can, show you're listening to what they're saying by referring to it: 'Oh dear – and when you were hurrying to get to your daughter's divorce party';
- You may have noticed that none of these examples of sympathy amounts to an apology. Being sympathetic does not mean you have to accept blame. The customer needs to get the problem off their chest before you necessarily have the chance to establish the cause of the problem. You need to give them sympathy before you know whether or not you owe them an apology;
- If it turns out that you *are* at fault in any way, apologise. You don't have to grovel, just say 'I'm very sorry the side panels were different lengths; that clearly shouldn't have happened. Let me put things right for you as soon as possible.' (A note of caution here: if the customer has suffered financial loss as a result of your negligence, you could be in trouble if you admit legal liability. But otherwise, it makes good customer relations sense. If in doubt, seek legal advice. There is a free legal advice number you can call if you are a member of the Federation of Small Businesses; see 'Useful Addresses');
- If it's not your fault, don't attempt to allocate blame. The customer is not going to warm to you if you tell them 'You must have put the shelves together wrongly.' Even if they have, you can tell them politely: 'It can be confusing if you haven't done it before...'

Take action to resolve the problem

- The customers' primary aim was to have their feelings acknowledged. Now you've done that they want the problem sorted out. You cannot sort out the problem until you know the facts. Sending someone round to assemble the shelves for them won't help if the pieces you sent don't fit together. Biking over a new shelf unit urgently may not be so ideal once you find out that they are in a different part of the country. So ask questions to establish all the relevant facts. Most people will understand this, but if they're impatient explain 'If you can just fill me in on a few details, it will help me to sort this out for you as quickly as possible. Can I take your address?'

- Now you have the facts, establish what the options are for putting the problem right: you could give the customer a refund, you could send them another side panel, you could send them another flat-packed shelf unit, you could assemble one for them and then send it and so on;

- Offer customers a choice; this way they feel they retain control of the solution. Once they have made a choice – albeit between only two options that you offered – it is their choice and they can't really argue with it. 'I can offer you a refund if you like, or I'll send you another shelf unit if you prefer. I can use a 24 hour carrier service, so you'll have it tomorrow.' If you have more than two options that you can offer, so much the better;

- Make sure it happens. This doesn't just mean phoning the carrier service and leaving a message for a colleague to package the unit up. It means following through and checking that it gets packaged up (maybe you should do it yourself), and making sure the carrier turns up to collect it on time.

Be efficient

- Follow all the guidelines we covered earlier for finding out people's names, message taking, calling people back, and so on;

- Give priority to resolving the complaint. Keep reminding yourself that every minute it takes makes customers less likely to buy from you again, and more likely to complain about you to their friends or colleagues;

- Keep customers in touch with what's going on. Always make contact when you said you would, and ring them to confirm what is happening;

- Contact the customer afterwards to make sure everything has gone smoothly: 'I'm just calling to check that your shelf unit arrived safely this morning. It did? Oh good. And everything's in order this time, I hope? Good. Thank you for letting us know about about the problems you were having; I'm glad we could sort things out for you.'

Did it work?

The question is, are you getting more repeat business? In other words, do your customers keep coming back? If the answer is yes, your customer care techniques are succeeding. In Chapter 6, we'll look at keeping customer records; one of their many uses is for measuring customer retention.

You can use the records to assess many of your customer care ideas. It may be hard to measure the precise value of each smile, but you can certainly see whether the customers you send thank-you gifts to are more likely to reorder. You could even test which is the best present to give them. Divide your list of loyal customers into two and send one thank-you gift to one half, and a different gift to the others. Then study their records after a few months and see if there is a significant difference between them. Or record which customers mentioned it and which didn't.

There's no such thing as perfect customer care – there's always room for improvement. So keep working on the techniques, make sure your staff do the same, and be on the lookout for new ideas constantly – whether they come from your customers, your staff, your competitors or anyone else.

Complaints

Keep a note of all the complaints you receive, along with details of how they were resolved. Obviously you will take note of them at the time, and if they are a symptom of a deeper problem you'll put that right. For example, if any customers complain that the machinery they bought from you has a faulty part, you will not only replace the part, you will also check to see how a faulty component could have got through the system.

In addition to this, however, you should go through the records regularly to see:

- whether the number of complaints is increasing or decreasing
- whether the customers who complain buy from you again
- which complaints crop up the most frequently

This final point is crucial. Identify the root cause of each complaint and make sure that as you tackle the problem, the number of complaints drops. Set yourself targets: next month, you will aim to reduce complaints to less than two a week, or whatever.

One other point: even if you don't think that the complaint was justified, you still need to record it. You may get several 'unjustified' complaints about the same thing. This means that, right or wrong, you have several unsatisfied customers. You must address these problems along with the rest. I'll give you an example. Suppose a customer rings up to complain that they can't assemble the flat-packed shelf unit you sent, because you haven't sent any screws with it. In fact, as you helpfully explain to them, you always tape the screws to the inside of the box for safe keeping and, if they have a look, they should find them there. That seems reasonable enough. But if six customers ring with this complaint, you must do something about it. You don't have to move the screws, but how about putting a note at the top of the instruction sheet saying: *You will find the screws taped to the inside of the box for safe-keeping in transit.*

6
SELLING

Selling is clearly a central part of marketing. You can do it through advertising, exhibiting, telemarketing or direct mail, all of which we'll look at later. Or you can do it face to face.

If you sell face to face there are two options:

1 the customer comes to you
2 you go to the customer

In this chapter, we'll focus on what happens when the customer comes to you. This covers any kind of retail selling, incoming telephone orders, and any type of business where the customer is already considering buying from you before the conversation starts.

The kind of face-to-face selling where you go to the customer is a fairly specialised skill. It is only a skill, and not a talent – which means that you can perfectly well learn it – but it would take more than a single chapter to tell you everything you need to know about buying signals and closing techniques and all the rest of it. If you sell your products or services in this way, you may already be an experienced sales person. If not, I recommend you buy one of the scores of books on the subject, and maybe enrol on a training course as well. Expensive as training can be, this is one area where it's virtually guaranteed to be money well spent. Having said all that, you should still find this chapter a very useful grounding in the subject, since all the basic rules of selling that it covers will apply to you as well.

There are certain skills you need to employ when you're selling, no matter who the customer and no matter what the product or service:

- talk in terms of benefits not features
- ask open questions
- listen to the customer
- never force a sale

This is not a chronological list of the process you go through in a sales conversation. You should practise all of these things all the time you are talking to the customer. We'll look at each of them in turn.

— Talk about benefits not features —

People don't buy products and services because of what they are; they buy them because of what they can do for them. We don't buy a bookshelf unit because it's made of pine and has four shelves. We buy it because it looks nice and will hold all the books we want to put on it. The fact that it's made of pine is the feature. The *benefit* is that it looks good and is the right size for our books. One feature can have several benefits, of course. The fact that it's made of pine might, to some people, be a benefit because that means it's tough, or that they can paint it easily, or that it's more environmentally friendly than mahogany.

The important thing is that you should focus on the benefits when you're selling to customers, not on the features. They don't want to know that your fax machines have a computer interface, but they do want to know that they can link them to the computer and use them as a printer as well as a fax. Even if they know what 'computer interface' means, they will still buy it for the benefit and not the feature. So you still need to talk to them in terms of benefits.

This is one of the most fundamental rules of selling, and one that many sales staff don't seem to understand. Which means that once you start doing it, you're already ahead of several of your competitors. I remember buying a cordless phone a few years ago. There were two models that seemed the same to me, at the same price, so I asked the sales assistant what the difference was. Her reply was 'This one has a call button, and that one doesn't.' I was none the wiser. I had never owned a cordless phone so I didn't know whether I wanted a call button, still not having a clue what it was. She had told me what the feature was, but she hadn't described the benefit. I wanted to know what the call button would do for me. She could have said, 'If you lose the handset, you can press this button on the base unit and the handset will ring, which will help you to find it.' These are both accurate answers to my question, but the second answer is far more likely to make me want to buy the phone.

EXERCISE

Here is a list of product and service features. Have a look through them and list the benefits that they provide. Bear in mind that some features have more than one possible benefit.

1 a 'last number redial' feature on a telephone

2 a car sunroof

3 a home collection laundry service

4 a grass collecting bag on a lawn mower

5 five star hotel accommodation on your holiday

Here are a few of the benefits you may have listed:

1 *a 'last number redial feature' on a telephone*

- it saves you time
- it saves you having to look up the last number again if you need to redial it

2 *a car sunroof*

- it means that you can stay cool in hot weather without a wind blowing through the car
- it lets more fresh air into the car
- it looks smart (people buy because of image benefits as well as practical ones)

3 *a home collection laundry service*

- saves you time going to the launderette
- saves you having to do a chore you don't enjoy

4 *a grass collecting bag on a lawn mower*

- it means you can keep the lawn tidier
- it saves you having to collect the clippings afterwards

5 *five star hotel accommodation on your holiday*

- you'll be really well looked after
- you'll be able to relax fully
- you'll feel spoilt
- you'll feel rich and important (if you're talking to a customer you will choose to phrase this a little differently – for example, 'you'll be rubbing shoulders with the best people').

There may well be other benefits for these products and services; I've just listed the obvious benefits. People may see all sorts of benefits that you hadn't anticipated. There's probably some amateur astronomer out there who wants a sunroof so they can stay in the car on cold nights while they're out stargazing, and still see the night sky when they look up. Or someone who wants a laundry service because they like the smell of commercial soap powder in the clothes when they get them back. So an important part of your job is to find out what benefits the customer wants – which is where the next two stages come in: asking open questions, and listening to the customer.

Ask open questions

If you want to know what customers want there's an obvious way to find out: ask them. But you have to ask them the right way. Suppose you're selling vacuum cleaners. Your sales conversation could go like this:

'Do you have any bare floorboards in the house?'
'No.'
'Do you have any thick pile carpets?'
'No.'
'Do you have many rugs?'
'No.'

This conversation is pretty heavy going. That's because the questions are all closed questions. That means that they require only a yes or no answer. It can take a long time to find out what you want to know. An open question requires a fuller answer. Open questions usually begin 'how', 'what' or 'why'. (If asking 'Why?' seems too pushy, you can replace it with 'what's the reason for...?') You could have replaced the conversation above with:

'How many different surfaces and carpet thicknesses do you have to vacuum?'
'They're all normal pile carpets, really.'

Open questions encourage people to open up and give fuller answers, because you can't answer simply yes or no to them. Here's another closed question which adds an additional problem:

'Do you do a lot of vacuuming?'
'Yes.'

That was certainly a closed question, but it was also misleading. How do you know that what you call a 'lot of vacuuming' is what they call a lot? Personally, I think that more than half an hour a year is a lot, but that might not be what the sales person is getting at. Why not ask an open question:

'How much vacuuming do you do?'
'About three hours a week.'

Now, doesn't that say more about whether or not they need a heavy duty cleaner?

———— Listen to the customer ————

It's not enough simply to ask the questions. You have to listen to the answers. Listen properly, and take them in fully. Don't make any assumptions about what customers want, or what benefits they need – they may want a benefit you haven't even thought of. Don't start telling them what good value for money this product is, when for all you know they may be millionaires desperate to get rid of all their money before they die so their grasping kids can't inherit it.

Just keep asking questions until you have a clear picture of what the customer is after, and choose the questions on the basis of what they have already told you. Use the customer's answers as a springboard for questions. For example: 'You said you have a three-storey house. Does that mean you'd like a lightweight model for carrying up and down stairs?' It's a good idea to follow what is known as the 80/20 rule: for the first 80 per cent of the conversation, you should do only 20 per cent of the talking. For the last 20 per cent – once you're clear what they want – you can do 80 per cent of the talking.

Let's go back to the vacuum cleaners. Suppose you sell around twenty different models. A customer comes in, or phones, and says 'I need a vacuum cleaner, but I'm not sure what kind.' Your job is to whittle your list of twenty down to one – the one the customer wants. You do this by asking open questions. By listening to the answers you can eliminate the vacuum cleaners on the list until you're left with the right one:

Stage 1
'How much vacuuming do you do?'
'About three hours a week.' (You can cross off the two extra-heavy- duty

models, and the two really lightweight models that are suited to occasional use only. You're down to sixteen.)

Stage 2
'How many different surfaces and carpet thicknesses do you have to vacuum?'
'They're all normal pile carpets really.' (You can cross off the three with special adaptors for adjusting the height – that leaves you with thirteen.)

Stage 3
'Is there anything else you want to use it for, apart from carpets, such as curtains or furniture?'
'I'd like to be able to use it to clean the curtains.' (You can cross off the five remaining models that don't have curtain brush attachments. Now you're down to nine.)

Stage 4
'What about small spaces such as behind furniture. How much will you be using the vacuum for that sort of cleaning?'
'Quite a lot; I don't want to have to keep bending down to clean things with a dustpan and brush – my back's not up to it these days.' (You can eliminate another five that don't have extensions for getting into small spaces. You're down to four and – if you were listening properly – you've learnt something else.)

Stage 5
'If you have a bad back, does that mean you'd prefer a lightweight model that's easier for you to carry around?'
'Oh yes. That's very important, now you mention it.' (Two more eliminated – that's just two left.)

Stage 6
'Where are you planning to store the vacuum cleaner when you're not using it?'
'It should just fit in the cupboard under the stairs – I hope I'm right about that!'
'So you'd like a slimline model?'
'Yes. It doesn't matter how tall it is, but it needs to be quite narrow.'
'I think you'd like this model here. It's lightweight and slimline, and it has attachments so you can use it to clean in tight spaces, and use it for curtains. It's designed for the amount of use you want out of it, so it will last well and shouldn't give you any trouble.'
'That sounds like just what I want.'

So you see, as soon as you start to listen your job becomes easy, and your customers go away satisfied, come back to buy from you again, and recommend you to other people.

Just one more point: don't introduce the question of price until they have. If you ask someone what their price range is they will give you a conservative estimate of what they want to spend. And if they've said they won't spend more than £80 it's a little difficult to start showing them models that cost £100. However, if they decide they like the £100 model before the question of price arises, they may well decide to buy it after all. This doesn't mean, however, that you should conceal the price from them – once they ask, you must tell them. However, you can soften the blow by telling them how much they will get for their money:

'It's £100, and that includes a three year parts warranty, all the attachments, two spare dustbags, free delivery if you live within ten miles, and even a plug already fitted on the end of the flex.'

—————— Never force a sale ——————

If you want any repeat business from your customers, or if you want them to recommend you to their colleagues or friends, don't ever push customers into making a purchase they don't really want. They may buy from you this time, but they won't dare come near you again for fear that they'll end up buying something else they don't want. How much better to have your customers think 'I'll ask in that vacuum cleaner shop, because if they haven't got what I want, they'll say so.'

The thing is, if you're asking open questions and listening to the answers, you can be certain that if you do sell what customers want, they'll buy from you. There's no chance that you won't realise what they're after.

—————— Expanding your sales ——————

Once you've made the sale, that's it. Isn't it? Well, not quite. Because you may have missed an opportunity to make *another* sale. There are two basic ways to do this:

1 find another product for the customer
2 find another customer for the product

Find another product or service for the customer

If you buy a pair of leather boots at a shoe shop, the sales assistant
will almost always ask you if you'd like to buy some leather cleaner to
go with them. Well, you can do the same. Offer your vacuum cleaner
customer extra accessories, perhaps, or some shake-on, vacuum-off
carpet freshener. Your customers may not know your full range of
products or services. If you're listening properly, you may pick up
clues that help you to keep them informed. Remember The Office
Plant Company, supplying plants to brighten up local companies'
reception areas and offices? Perhaps while you're delivering plants to
one of your new customers, they might say:

'We could do with some plants in the showroom as well, but it's going
to be more than enough work just looking after this lot.'

This gives you the opportunity to respond:

'We operate a maintenance service as well. I could call in twice a
week and water and tidy up the plants for you. Shall I put together a
quote for you?'

Sometimes, you may get an enquiry for something you don't sell.
Instead of simply saying 'I'm sorry, we don't sell that. You could try
the electrical supplies' shop down the road', consider whether you sell
a different product or service that would do just as well. You may
need to find out what benefit the customer wants in order to establish
whether you can help them. Here's an example:

'Do you sell vacuum cleaners with turbo suction?'
'Can I ask why you're after a turbo suction?'
'Well, I have a couple of thick pile carpets and I want a vacuum that
will be able to suck the dust up really thoroughly, even though it's
deeper down.'
'We don't have a turbo suction model, but this one here has a special
thick pile setting which uses an increased suction power to clean carpets
deeper down.'
'Oh. That would probably do just as well, actually.'

I once asked at a well-known high street store (which I shan't name)
whether they sold coathangers. 'Sorry, no' was the assistant's reply.
As I was leaving, I spotted a rack of them. I took them to the cash
desk to pay for them. While I was there, I asked the assistant, 'Why

did you tell me that you didn't sell coathangers?' She informed me: 'We don't. Those aren't coathangers. They're trouser hangers.'

Find another customer for the product or service

Have you ever bought anything mail order from a catalogue? You may well have filled out a form that had a section saying: 'Do you know anyone else who would like to receive a copy of our catalogue? Just fill in their name and address here...' If you run a mail order business, try it. But you can do it in other kinds of business, too. Simply ask your satisfied customers if they can recommend anyone else who you could send a brochure to (they're not going to volunteer their friends for a hard-sell routine). Or ask them to take copies of your brochure to pass on.

This way of expanding your sales is particularly effective if you sell to businesses. If you're confident that a customer is satisfied with the service they get from you, simply ask them 'Is there anyone else in the company who might want a few plants to brighten up their office?' Business people will be a lot less worried than private customers about passing contact names on to you.

— Using someone else to sell for you —

Would you be better off selling through an agent, a wholesaler/distributor or a retailer? It depends on a number of things:

- what your product or service is
- how difficult your product is to distribute
- what your administration costs are
- your profit margins
- your own selling skills
- your personal time restrictions.

Selling through someone else has various pros and cons:

Pros	Cons
• It frees up your time spent selling;	• You lose control of how your customers are treated;

- It frees up your time spent on admin;
- In a specialist market, the agent or distributor will already have contacts;
- It is less risky/expensive than taking on a full time sales person;

- If the agent/distributor doesn't feel excited about your product, they won't push it as hard as you would;
- They take a percentage of your profits;
- They may well want more promotional material and brochures than you would need if you were selling the product or service yourself.

Bearing all that in mind, you should be able to work out for yourself whether you'd be better off selling through a third party. Remember that you have the option to use someone else for certain things only:

- for some products or services only
- for selected parts of the country
- for selected sectors of the market (business-to-business clients only, for example)
- for overseas sales.

Which kind of third party?

You'll need to know what the difference is between an agent, a wholesaler/distributor and a retailer before you know which you want to use.

An agent sells on your behalf without actually being an employee. They pass orders back to you and you fulfill them and invoice the customer direct. You pay the agent a commission, which is usually between 7.5 per cent and 15 per cent. You need to agree with an agent, in writing, that they will not sell your competitors' products, and in exchange you will have to guarantee not to sell direct to any of their contacts. It can be hard for a small firm to find a good agent; they will often refuse to take you on unless they can see a real potential for growth in your business.

A wholesaler/distributor is a customer – a big customer. You sell direct to them and they add a mark-up, which can be as high as 100 per cent. Your turnover will be lower, but so will your costs in terms of selling and distribution. If you use distributors you'll have a few large customers instead of a lot of smaller customers. This can leave you very vulnerable if the wholesaler/distributor stops buying from you, unless you are selling through several of them.

A retailer is a kind of halfway house between using a distributor and doing your own selling. If you make a retail product, a distributor will be selling it on to retailers. If you cut out this middle stage, you'll get a higher price from the retailers. On the other hand, you'll have more customers (a wholesaler will sell on to several retailers), which means that you have higher distribution costs, and so on.

Choosing an agent, distributor or retailer

Before you can choose someone to do your selling for you, you've got to know how to find them. In the United Kingdom there are two national bodies that carry lists of agents: the British Agents' Register, and the Manufacturers' Agents Association (see 'Useful Addresses'). Wholesalers/distributors and retailers will be listed in *Yellow Pages*, *The Thomson Directory* and so on, under the product category.

If you're exhibiting, you can hang a sign on your stand saying 'agents/distributors wanted'. Another excellent way of finding agents and distributors is to talk to the retailers who stock your products and ask them for a recommendation.

Once you have found a few possible candidates, you need to select the best. Ask them all:

- Who else they sell on behalf of (if they are agents) or whose lines they stock (if they are wholesalers);
- What their sales record is (if they are good at selling, and reliable, they should be happy to show you some evidence of their turnover).

In the case of agents, you will also want to make sure:

- They are already selling to the right industry (though not selling competing products). For example, if you manufacture animal feeds you want an agent who sells to farmers. You don't want them to be selling someone else's feed, but if they're selling milking machines, that's fine;
- They have enough good contacts. Ask them, and ask a few questions to make sure they know the industry well enough, too;
- They put across the right image for your business. The customers will judge you by the person who does your selling for you.

Did it work?

It's pretty obvious whether your selling is working or not – what has happened to your turnover? However, to keep it working you need to know which bits worked best, and why. Otherwise you might be pumping money into certain products or services, certain customers, or certain sales approaches that are not as cost effective as you think. If this is the case, you should be even more profitable than you are. And it always is the case, sooner or later. Customers and markets change and if you aren't monitoring yours, you won't be able to make the most of the changes.

The answer is simple: keep records of everything. A computer is ideal for this but if you haven't invested in one yet you can use a traditional card index file just as well. So what should you record? Keep a card or a computer entry for each customer, and note down:

- the customer's full details including name, address, phone and fax numbers and e-mail address
- for business customers, record the names and job titles of all your contacts
- for business (and sometimes domestic) customers, record the type of business or type of customer
- every transaction, including the details of the order and the date, and who placed the order if you have more than one contact at the same address
- a history of payments, including when they paid
- a history of any problems or complaints, including how they were resolved
- details of any sales visits or phone calls to the customer

In the United Kingdom, if you keep these details on a computer you will have to register under the Data Protection Act (the address of the Data Protection Registrar is in 'Useful Addresses').

This means you can check virtually any detail of your selling record by cross-referencing these various factors. A computer obviously helps here, but you can manage without. Suppose you phone each of your customers every three months to make contact and give them the opportunity to place a fresh order. Business is going well and your customer list is expanding. It's becoming harder to find the time to make these calls. Are they worthwhile? Would once every six months do? How can you know?

You can look at your customer records, that's how. How many of your customers order during or shortly after this phone call? How many seem to order every other phone call? Is it always the same customers who place an order when you ring? If you experiment by reducing these calls to twice yearly for some of your customers, will your sales drop? These questions – and many more – will be answered by your sales records. So keep them. What's more, they will help you with research, advertising, direct mail and virtually every other aspect of your business, too.

7

EXHIBITIONS

If you're tempted to skip this chapter – hold on a moment. Many small businesses feel that they don't need to go to exhibitions and trade shows, but often they would benefit hugely if they did. As a guideline: if you don't have a shop front, or you do but you also sell by phone, mail order or face-to-face visits, this chapter is for you.

Do you think trade shows and exhibitions are money-losers or money-spinners? Whatever your opinion – you're right. It depends entirely on how you go about exhibiting. If you do it badly, it's one of the most effective ways there is to throw your money away. But if you do it well, exhibiting is one of the most cost-effective selling techniques you'll ever use. This chapter is about how to make sure that you do it well; before, during and after the actual exhibition itself.

—— Planning and preparation ——

The first question to ask yourself is 'Why?' What are the objectives you hope to achieve by exhibiting? If you ask exhibitors what they are doing at a show, you'll get a wide range of answers. Many of them will tell you that they are collecting new leads, or publicising a new product launch. These are good reasons for attending. Many exhibitors, however, have only the vaguest purpose: 'to show the flag' or 'because we always exhibit at this show.' These are probably the same people who are tempted to think that exhibiting is a waste of money. It is, unless you have a clear reason for being there.

You must, first and foremost, know why you are planning to attend a show. Exhibiting – at trade shows, craft fairs, agricultural shows or business-to-business exhibitions – can achieve a number of objectives:

- introduce you to new prospects (especially if you're expanding into new geographical or product areas)
- reinforce relationships with existing customers whom you rarely meet
- publicise a new product or service launch
- help you to break into a new market
- help you find agents and distributors, at home or overseas
- give you a lot of customer feedback in a short time, on existing or planned products or services
- act as a lucrative outlet for your goods

As I said at the start, unless you have a shop front and don't sell through any other route, you are virtually bound to want to achieve at least one of these objectives, if not several. Now it's just a matter of finding the right exhibition to achieve your objective.

EXERCISE

This is the first part of a two-part exercise. You'll find the second part on page 109. (This is the easy half, by the way.) List what your key objectives in exhibiting might be. There may be only one, but it's likely there will be more.

KEY OBJECTIVES

Choosing the right show

This is one of the most crucial aspects of exhibiting. But for some reason, huge numbers of business people (not only from small businesses
like yours, but also from those big enough to know better) don't start
thinking about what they're doing until *after* they have made this
decision. How they decide I haven't a clue – I suppose they just attend
the nearest exhibition, or the exhibitions they have heard of, or
maybe they pick names out of a hat.

In any case, attending the *right* shows is crucial, at least for small
companies who can't afford to chuck money away. So which are the
right shows? The answer is simple. Who do you want to meet there?
Your objectives should tell you this. Do you want to meet new
prospects? Existing customers? Potential agents and distributors?
Overseas agents? Find out which shows they visit, and exhibit there.

Be original about working out who you want to meet, by the way.
Exhibitions give you an ideal opportunity to meet people you'd never
meet otherwise – not in a concentrated group, anyway. If you want to
meet your existing customers, that's one thing. But suppose you want
to reach new customers? If you produce high quality regional food –
smoked venison and cider-roast ham, say – you are probably selling to
retail outlets and direct to consumers by mail order. How about going
to a regional business trade show for marketing managers and directors? You could promote hampers of your produce as ideal upmarket
Christmas gifts for them to give to their top customers.

Who goes where?

You're looking for high numbers of the right kind of visitors. So the
next question is: how do you know which shows these people visit?
There are plenty of ways to find out.

First of all, have a look at *Exhibition Bulletin*. This lists exhibitions
and trade shows around the United Kingdom. After all, you can't find
out who visits which exhibitions until you know which exhibitions
exist. You should find a copy of *Exhibition Bulletin* in your nearest
main library, or you can contact the publishers (the address is at the
back of the book). If you can't afford an annual subscription you can
buy a single copy, which lists exhibitions up to about 18 months
ahead. Or why not split the cost with other local business people who

are thinking of exhibiting? *Exhibition Bulletin* lists well over a thousand UK exhibitions a year, from local craft shows attracting 200 visitors to huge international shows with hundreds of thousands of visitors. It also includes overseas shows, which may be useful if you do a lot of exporting.

Armed with this information, you now want to select the exhibitions which seem reasonably promising. If all your customers are local, you can concentrate on local shows. If you are in the engineering trade, you can focus on the specialist engineering shows, and so on.

This should give you a shortlist of exhibitions that are relevant to your business. Now you will need to decide which of them you will visit. If you have never exhibited before it's wise not to commit yourself to too many shows until you've attended one or two and found out how effective they are for you. The lessons you learn will help you to select the best shows to attend after that. So how do you narrow this shortlist down to the one or two most promising shows? Here are a few ideas:

- Contact a sample of the people you want to meet (customers, prospects, agents or whoever) and ask them which shows they attend. They won't mind – people are always flattered to be asked for their opinion or advice;
- Contact non-competing companies which sell to the same market as you and ask them which shows they find the most useful. For example, if you're selling local, high quality meat produce, get in touch with a local wine and cider producer, or someone who sells upmarket chutneys and pickles;
- Contact the exhibition organisers; any reputable organiser will tell you what you want to know. Ask them:
  - the number of exhibitors at their shows for the last three years
  - the number of visitors for the last three years, with a break down if possible (i.e. how many buyers, how many marketing managers, how many MDs and so on)
  - whether they give exhibitors a list of who has visited the show, after the event

  In addition, ask the organisers to send you a copy of last year's catalogue, an application form, a list of exhibitors who have already booked for the next show, details of prices, and so on.

It is a good idea to visit a show before you book space at it. Since, as we shall see later on, you should give yourself several months to prepare for an exhibition, it will rarely be a problem to visit it this year and then consider attending next year.

Is it worth the cost?

Remember those objectives I was talking about a couple of pages ago? Well, you have to be a little more specific about them to establish whether it will be cost-effective to visit the shows that are left on your list. You need to know how many new leads you aim to pick up, and what their value will be to you. Or the turnover you expect to make from selling venison and cider-roast ham direct to the public at the Bath & West agricultural show. Or the financial value of finding an overseas agent (in other words, the value of all the orders they'll bring in from Germany or Indonesia or Lapland). To give you a clue, you can reckon that around 10 to 20 per cent of the total visitors will visit your stand (that is if it's positioned and designed properly, which we'll look at later). You should have some idea, from the customer records we looked at in Chapter 6, what your conversion rate is. In other words, what percentage of prospects usually 'convert' into actual customers.

EXERCISE

Here's the second half of the exercise you started on page 105. This time, list your key objectives in the left-hand column. List your corresponding specific objectives, and their value, in the other two columns. If you still have several exhibitions on your shortlist, it's worth going through this exercise for each one (the centre and right hand columns will change according to the number of visitors you expect at the show).

Next, you need to know what it will cost you to attend the exhibition. In addition to the cost of the stand and the space, you should allow for display material, extra brochures and other literature, advance promotion, staff costs, travel and accommodation.

Now put the two sets of figures together. If the costs are greater than the anticipated profit, forget it. Cross that show off your list. If the profits are greater than the costs, that's good. But there's another calculation to do before you fill in your application form and send off your cheque.

Suppose your objective is to generate new leads. Divide your total costs by the total number of people you expect to visit your stand. Suppose the total cost for a modest stand at a local show is £1,000, including staff time, promotion and everything else. Let's say there

Exhibition:		
Key objectives	**Specific objectives**	**Value**

are likely to be around 800 visitors. If 15 per cent of them visit your stand, that's 120 visitors. So divide £1000 (the total cost) by 120 (visitors to your stand) and you have the cost per contact: £8.33.

It's costing you £8.33 per face-to-face meeting with a contact. How does that compare with the alternatives, such as setting up appointments to visit their office, or sending them all a mailshot? You have to know this to know whether it is cost-effective to exhibit. The answer is often yes; it costs a fortune to keep a sales person on the road. A mailshot good enough to generate the same number of leads could be expensive – a mailing list that good wouldn't come cheap.

If you're not trying to generate leads, try an equivalent calculation. If your objective is to collect market research information, what would it cost to do this by any other means? If you want to find an overseas agent, what would it cost to meet them all otherwise?

By the time you've completed all these stages, you should have identified the best one or two exhibitions to attend. If by any chance there is no exhibition that seems worthwhile when you do your calculations, don't exhibit. But keep on the lookout. New shows are being started up all the time, and if you can only find the right one you'll have found yourself an ideal low-cost method of selling.

Planning the stand

There are three main stages to planning the stand: choosing where in the exhibition venue you want to be, deciding what type and size of stand you want, and designing the display itself.

Choosing the site

The difference between a good and a bad location can make a huge difference to the number of visitors who pass your stand – a well placed stand can attract several times more visitors than a badly placed stand. Past exhibitors tend to get first choice, but if you book well in advance (a year or more for a large show), you'll obviously get a better choice than if you book when most of the best locations have been taken.

Here are the key points to consider when selecting a site:

- Visitors often shoot straight past the stands near the entrance in their eagerness to get into the thick of the exhibition;
- People often miss out stands that you would expect them to visit last because they run out of time, or just get tired. This includes stands near the exit and stands that are towards the end of any logical route round the venue;
- Stands round the edge are the most visited – people have to pass them to get to the bar, the toilets, the entrances and exits, the workshop and seminar locations, and so on;
- Facing down an aisle is a good spot, because visitors can see you long before they reach you;
- Corner locations are particularly good. The further the stand can be seen from, the better, and a corner site can be seen down more than one aisle;

- Avoid sites opposite exhibitors whose stands are particularly exciting – with glamorous models or dramatic visual effects – because no one will notice you. When you book, ask the organiser who has booked already and avoid those that you know from experience will steal the show (you will obviously get better over time at recognising who these companies are);
- You could do worse than site yourself near to a competitor who is much bigger than you, because they will attract the right visitors to your part of the venue, and you will get the benefit of their pre-publicity as well as your own. In one survey, over three-quarters of visitors said that a key reason for visiting exhibitions was to compare products from different potential suppliers.

Choosing the stand

You can book one of two types of exhibition space: a 'shell stand', which is a basic stand with wall panels, fascia boards and name boards, identical to all the other shell stands at the show; or 'space only', which is cheaper, but you have to supply the stand yourself. Either way, you will have to provide your own display materials, of course.

If you are exhibiting for the first time, you would probably be better off taking a shell stand (unless you are lucky enough to know someone from whom you can borrow a suitable stand). If you subsequently find that exhibiting is profitable for you and you plan to do it quite often, it will probably be worth investing in your own stand and renting space only. Having your own stand gives you a greater choice of design and a more individual image.

The size of stand you go for is bound to be largely determined by cost. However, there can come a point where it simply isn't worth exhibiting if the only space you can afford is too small. You'll have to redo your costings, estimating fewer visitors. If you can't afford a decent site, enough wall space for your display, or enough floor space to demonstrate your product, you should think about whether to increase your budget or whether to miss the show.

The other point to bear in mind is the question of image that we covered in Chapter 3. What will it say about you if your stand is small and poky, while your competitors all have huge, glamorous stands? In some lines of business it really won't matter, as long as your stand is smart and presentable, but in others it will. It's a matter of whether your customers want to know that their suppliers are large and success-ful, or whether they are more concerned with quality, or price, or service.

Designing the display

Your biggest competitors will be going to specialist exhibition design-ers to create the best possible stand. You, on the other hand, can't afford to. Your options are:

- to use a graphic designer, at least for some parts of the design
- to approach college design departments and see if a student designer will take on the job for a small fee as a project
- to use a signwriter for one or two key parts of the design
- to do the job yourself, or persuade the more artistic of your long-suffering friends to help you out

The important thing is that the design should be up to the appropriate standard for the exhibition you are attending. If you're selling office sup-plies to business buyers at a large regional trade show, a home-made sign will look appallingly tacky and out of place. But if you're selling hand printed silk scarves at a local craft fair, it could look just right.

Make sure that your stand reflects the image you want to put across, and follows through your corporate identity (see Chapter 3). Whoever designs your stand, there are certain guidelines to follow. Here are the ten key rules for exhibition stand design:

1 Attract people's attention. You're competing with tens or even hun-dreds of other stands, so you must do something pretty special to get people to notice yours. Make the display eye-catching, and make sure that *something is going on* all the time. The experts always say that you must have something moving: a working model of a product (that is moving constantly); a craftsperson actu-ally spinning, turning wood or whatever; a video running or some-thing of the sort. Food cooking, if you're in the right business and the right exhibition, is another big draw. There are certain guide-lines you must follow, however, to make this technique work well:
   - It must be relevant to your business. It's no good having a flashing light display or a working model of a roller-coaster without a good reason;
   - The moving display must be big enough to attract attention, but not so huge it swamps the stand. Don't put moving displays where the first visitor to the stand will obscure them;

- Remember that anyone who is busy operating a working model or making cricket bats is not going to be available to encourage people on to the stand;
- Consider the safety implications. Don't have trailing wires for people to trip over, or machines with moving parts they can get their fingers stuck in. Visitors at exhibitions are like small children –they want to touch everything. (The only difference is, they tend to have more money than small children, so encourage them to do whatever they like.)
- If a product is new, have a big sign that says 'New'. The majority of visitors are actively looking for new products – that's why they are there.

2 Let the visitor know what's in it for them. In other words, sell the *benefit* of stopping to talk (we looked at benefits in Chapter 6). You could do this with a display sign, the smell of bacon cooking, or – a popular method – by running a draw or a competition (this has another benefit, too, because it gives you an opportunity to take their name and address; we'll consider that aspect of it later in the chapter);

3 Any display materials should be simple to follow, and easy to see and read. Don't print text on to display boards at knee-height. Headlines should be a little above head height, and text should be as close to eye level as possible. Print labels and signs, don't type them;

4 Make sure there is plenty of room for you, your visitors and any display materials or equipment on the stand. If any serious prospect is going to want to stop and talk for a few minutes, you should do your best to find room for a couple of easy chairs as well;

5 Don't create any psychological barriers that will deter visitors from 'coming on board', such as a leaflet dispenser at the front of the stand, or a step up. A carpet can encourage people to step across – the easiest way to provide this is to buy carpet tiles which you can stack up and store fairly easily from one exhibition to the next. You can also replace any stained or damaged tiles;

6 Decide which products you are going to promote. You won't necessarily have room for your whole range on display, especially if you make four poster beds, wardrobes, dining tables and sofas, and your stand is only 2 metres square;

7 Allowing for the point I've just made, display your product if you possibly can. Let the visitors see it, touch it, watch it working, taste it or anything else they want to do with it. If it won't fit on

the stand, have a model of it – or a slide sequence or video or photograph. If you can't fit a four poster bed on the stand, how about catching people's attention by building *half* a four poster bed? They can still feel the wood and judge the quality of the craftsmanship;

8 Display plenty of literature about your products or services;

9 Make sure your stand is well lit, and make the lighting as interesting and attractive as possible. Don't have it shining straight into your eyes – you'll regret it within the first couple of hours;

10 Build into the design a space to store your coats, bags, spare brochures and so on. And remember that exhibitions are notorious for thieves, so make sure the space is well tucked away at the back of the stand.

Pulling in the punters

The exhibition organisers, if they are doing their job properly, will publicise the event in advance and try to attract as many visitors as possible. This is deceptively appealing, to the point where over three-quarters of exhibitors (according to some research) leave them to get on with it. Don't. No matter how good a job they do, they are not trying to attract people to your stand. They are trying to attract them to the show in general.

Most exhibitors wait by their displays hoping that their customers, potential customers or whoever they want to see just happen to be visiting the show. And, since not every visitor necessarily goes round the whole show – especially a large one – they hope that if the people they want to meet *do* visit the show, they will chance to walk past their stand.

Well, you can do better than that. You can put yourself in the most professional 20 to 25 per cent of all exhibitors by telling people in advance that you're going to be there. Those visitors I mentioned who don't go round the whole exhibition: the reason is that they don't need to, because they know where they're going. They're heading for the suppliers who contacted them in advance saying 'Come and see us, we'll be on stand D14.'

Who should you tell?

There's not a lot of point in telling your London customers that you're going to be exhibiting in Belfast (unless it's a huge exhibition that attracts visitors from that far afield). So contact people who are in the catchment area of the exhibition. Of those, you need to inform some or all of the following:

- existing customers
- prospects
- agents and distributors
- general public

How should you tell them?

There are various ways you can make contact, and the most appropriate will depend on who and where the customers and prospects are. You will often find that it pays to reach people through more than one medium, since it increases the chance of their noticing and remembering.

Just because someone knows that you'll be at the exhibition, it doesn't automatically mean that they'll feel there's any need to visit you. You need to tell them what's in it for them. A chance to sample some smoked venison, or to see your latest product or service. So when you contact them, make sure you give them a good reason to come and see you. You could even send out vouchers to be redeemed at your stand: 'Exchange this voucher for two free game pies at The Devon Pantry, stand D14', and include the date and venue so they don't forget. Many show organisers will also give you tickets to send out.

Here are a few more ways to reach people:

- The exhibition publicity machine: the organisers run editorial coverage in their catalogue, and put out press releases to the local or trade press. They will feature your business only if you give them press releases and other information. Make the most of this opportunity; most companies – especially the smaller companies – don't;
- Mailshot: write to your customers or prospects inviting them to come and visit your stand. Chapters 8 and 9 will give you more ideas on how to identify prospects;
- Advertising: you may find that it pays to advertise in the trade press, or locally if you're aiming to attract the general public. Chapter 8 will look at advertising in detail;
- Local and trade press: contact them well in advance to see whether they are running a special feature on the exhibition. The deadline for press releases or ads could be as much as six months ahead of time;

- Posters: for a local show which aims to attract the general public, a poster campaign may be effective. You can put posters on buses or billboards, in your shop, on your van or in the shop windows of your retail outlets;
- Newsletter: if you run a customer newsletter, publicise your attendance at exhibitions;
- Word-of-mouth: the further ahead you plan your exhibition presence, the more chance you have to publicise it this way. For months before the exhibition you could be telling your hotel industry prospects 'We don't sell speciality pies at the moment, but we'll be introducing a range next autumn. We're going to launch them at the Newcastle Catering Show, so come along and sample them.'

The practical planning details

There are plenty of practical details that you need to consider when you exhibit. They shouldn't be a problem, or even particularly time consuming, but you *must* consider them well in advance. Otherwise you could create huge problems that could have been avoided altogether if only you'd spent a few minutes checking out the details.

I won't go through the complete list, because it varies so much from show to show, but I'll give you a couple of examples. Many organisers won't allow you to use materials on your stand that are not fire retardant. Simple if you know before you design the stand; potentially catastrophic if you don't find out until you turn up on the day of the show and they won't let you use your display materials. Here's another one: you generally have to let the organisers know well in advance how many electric sockets you're going to need. If you don't read the small print until it's too late, you may have no way of making your expensive working model move. So read the small print when you apply for the exhibition space, and make notes of anything relevant. Also, mark in your diary any dates by which you have to notify the organisers if you want to use something, or pay, or send in the entry to go in the catalogue, and so on.

There are other things you will need to consider in plenty of time as well. Here are the most important:

- arranging transport to the exhibition for your display and equipment
- arranging accommodation if necessary

- organising design and printing of advance publicity material (this may be as little as a handful of posters, but it still needs to be planned in plenty of time)
- organising extra sales literature to hand out on the stand (You can get through huge numbers of brochures at an exhibition – some visitors seem to collect them. On a limited budget you can print some inexpensive brochures, and hand out your normal, more expensive brochures only to promising visitors.)
- preparing extra stock to take with you if you're going to be selling direct from the stand
- preparing for the potential influx of orders that may follow the exhibition.

The big day

You're almost there. If you've done everything right so far, you're well on the way to a thoroughly successful exhibition. There are just two more things you have to attend to, once the exhibition is underway: persuading the people who stop and look at your stand to go that little bit further and talk to you, and then making sure that you fully exploit the opportunities offered to you.

Encouraging visitors

There are tens, or even hundreds, of stands at the exhibition. No one has time to visit them all. As they go round the venue, the visitors are unconsciously – or perhaps even consciously – rationing themselves. 'Shall I visit that one? No, maybe not. What about that one... I'm not sure, really..' and so on. When they get to your stand, you want them to think – unconsciously – 'Ah! That one looks worth a closer look...' We've already examined the design factors that will encourage this response, but we also need to consider how you, and anyone else on the stand, behaves. The non-verbal messages have a huge effect.

The first thing is that there should be more than one of you on the stand. Even if you're running a business on your own, drag one of those poor friends of yours along. Running an exhibition stand is the most tiring thing in the world – it's more exhausting than climbing Everest (I've only tried one of them, but I just know). However exhausting you think it will be, it's worse. Even if you've done it before – it's worse than you remember.

You can't possibly hide your exhaustion from the visitors. You might manage it for the first few hours, but you won't by the end of the day. And a slumped, yawning exhibitor isn't going to encourage anyone to do business with you. And even if you *still* don't believe how exhausting it is, imagine your best prospect wandering past your stand when there's nobody there, because you had to go to the lavatory, or thought you'd take advantage of the lull to go and fetch a cup of coffee. No, you simply must have someone else there, even if only to wander up and give you a break once every couple of hours.

The next thing is that everyone on the stand must be trained – including the friend who is helping out. They should be trained in your business and product range, so they can answer questions, and they should be trained in exhibition stand techniques. The most important of these techniques are:

- Dress in a way that fits with the image we looked at in Chapter 3;
- Look welcoming. Don't slump in the chairs or lounge against the displays. Don't stand blocking the front of the stand with your arms folded. Don't look as though you're going to pounce on people the moment they step onto the stand. Don't natter in a little clique with your colleagues. Look relaxed and discreet, and be ready with a warm smile;
- Once visitors step on to the stand, give them a moment or two to themselves; you may frighten them off if you pounce too soon. Then approach (before they have time to simply wander off) and start a conversation. If you say 'Can I help you?' they are likely to say 'No' which leaves you with little room for manouevre. So ask them open questions (as we saw in Chapter 6). Relate these to your product, and try to tie it in with whatever they are looking at at the time. If they're looking at your Christmas hampers, ask 'What sort of Christmas gifts do you give your customers at the moment?'
- Make the stand look welcoming. At the start of the show, this will happen automatically. But by the end, especially if the show goes on for a few days, it will be littered with coffee cups and discarded brochures and broken bits of the display. Don't let this happen;
- Arrange brochures and leaflets to look neat, but don't make them too perfect. If you spend hours fanning them out perfectly, people won't want to take one for fear of disrupting your display.

Making it all worthwhile

So you had between 150 and 250 visitors to your stand who actually chatted to you, and quite a few seemed very interested. You'll be expecting a few enquiries and orders in the next few weeks as a result of that! Pretty good, eh? No, actually. You should be able to say *exactly* how many people visited your stand, *and* who they all were, and *you* should be contacting *them* over the next few weeks. Unless you attended the show only to sell to people you never intend to sell to again, you should have all this information – and more – at your fingertips by the end of the show.

You should get the contact details of every serious prospect who visits your stand. If they have a genuine interest, they won't mind giving you the details. Early on in the conversation, say 'May I ask your name?' Then ask their company, if you're selling to businesses (they'll probably give you a business card before you get that far). Apart from anything else, until you find out who they are, you could be talking to one of your competitors trying to pick up a few things you'd rather they didn't know (exhibitions are prime places for doing this). Or this could be one of your best customers, and you're treating them as if they know nothing about your products.

If you're selling to the public, ask for their address. If you want an excuse to do this, make sure there's some kind of literature that you don't have on the stand – such as a detailed specification of individual products in the range. Then you can tell them you want their address so you can send the information on to them. If they're genuinely interested, they'll give it to you.

You may want to collect large numbers of names and addresses of anyone visiting the show. This will give you a large but less targeted mailing list. For some products, this could well be what you want. If you sell personal organisers, for example, just about everyone visiting a business-to-business show will be a potential customer. In this case, you may want to run a competition or a draw. Everyone has to give you their contact details, or how could you contact them to let them know if they've won? Offer a free personal organiser to the person whose name you draw on the last day of the show.

Keeping a record

You should have a record book, preferably with an A–Z divider. Everyone working on your stand should record the contact details of everyone they speak to, along with notes of what sales literature they gave them and what follow-up action you should take. And any other remarks that are relevant. For business exhibitions you should also keep an index file to drop business cards into. It saves time to write notes on the back of these if there's room. Otherwise have a stapler handy to staple them into the record book and write notes beside them (don't paper clip them or they'll become detached and you'll never marry up the notes and the cards later.

These records are the most valuable thing on your stand. I don't care about the £3000 worth of four poster bed, or the credit cards in your wallet. The records are worth more. Do not lose them. They could be the means to sell another two dozen four poster beds for you. They must not fall out of your briefcase, be forgotten at the end of the day, or be left lying around to be stolen by unscrupulous competitors (I'm afraid it does happen).

Following up

Now you have this information: use it. You may well have agreed follow up contact with some of these leads: 'I'll put that brochure in the post to you next week', 'I'll call you to fix an appointment' and so on. But you should contact the rest of them as well. You can do this by phone, post, fax, e-mail or by face-to-face visits – whatever suits your business and the number of leads there are to follow up.

Enter as much information as you can on your customer records (which we covered at the end of Chapter 6). This applies to existing customers who visited you, and new prospects – open new entries for them. That way you'll be able to tell how you met them. One survey (specifically of trade shows) indicated that the average length of time it took to convert a lead into a sale was seven months, and it could take as long as two years. If you haven't recorded the contact in your records, how will you know, when the order for 500 cider-baked hams finally comes through, that you first met this new customer at the Newcastle Catering Show? And if you don't know that, how will you know whether it's worth exhibiting at the Newcastle Catering Show again?

Did it work?

It's very easy to assess the effectiveness of exhibitions. After all, you set yourself a clear objective right at the start; did you meet it? If so, the exhibition was successful.

However, it's always worth analysing your results in a bit more depth, to see if you can do even better next time. So ask yourself:

- What were the most successful aspects, and why: did you attract a high proportion of people on to the stand? Did you sell more than you expected to? Did you meet more customers than you had anticipated?
- What were the least successful aspects, and why: did people tend to walk straight past your stand? Were the visitors the wrong type of people? Were there fewer agents there than you had expected?
- What else could you have done that you didn't? If you don't think about this straight away, and make a note of it, you may have forgotten by the time you come to do the next show. Often something strikes you once you get to the show, or you notice something one of the other exhibitors is doing. For instance, you might realise that if you sell hot food as well as cold (venison sausages, or grilled duck wings wrapped in smoked bacon) the smell will attract more people to your stand.

Finally, don't make the mistake of trundling off to the same show again next year, and the year after, just because it worked this time. Set your objective clearly and do the costings, and decide whether or not to attend on the same methodical basis every time.

8

ADVERTISING

The key to effective advertising – like so many aspects of marketing – is to target your audience as accurately as possible. You can't afford to advertise to fifty thousand people who will never buy your product, just because there will be a few hundred amongst them who might become customers – *if* they read the ad. And yet that is exactly what countless small businesses do every time they place an ad in the local weekly newspaper. You need to find a way of reaching those few hundred only, because then every pound you spend will be worthwhile.

Few small businesses have a clear advertising plan. They don't really know where to advertise, or when, or how. They either do no advertising at all, or they put an ad in the local paper or the trade press because they feel they 'ought to'. They are easy prey for the advertising sales staff at the local paper, who all too often talk them into wasting their money on a misplaced ad. But they don't know they have wasted their money, because they don't know how to judge whether the ad is successful or not.

However, that's other small business owners, not you. Because by the time you've finished reading this chapter you'll know exactly when to advertise, and where, and how – and why.

Why advertise?

This is the first and most important question. 'In order to sell more' is the answer many people give. That's not unreasonable, but you have to be sure that you *will* sell more as a result. Even if you do, there's the possibility that if you had invested the money in some other form of selling, you might have had a greater return.

I'll give you a genuine example of this. A West Country hotel owner wanted to promote his hotel as a great place for fishing enthusiasts to stay, because the grounds included several hundred yards of river frontage with fishing rights. He thought, like most small business people, that he had better place a few ads. The obvious publications were specialist fishing magazines. But he found that the cost was far more than he could afford.

So he tried another approach. He decided to find out what sort of people go fishing. In the course of researching this, he made the unexpected discovery that 70 per cent of GPs like to fish in their spare time. But where is the best place to advertise to GPs? The answer to this turned out to be not to advertise at all. Instead, the hotel owner took a stand at an exhibition of medical supplies and equipment. Not only was this cheaper than advertising in fishing magazines or exhibiting at a show for anglers, but it had the huge added advantage that his was the only hotel represented there. It brought in more business (and still does) than an ad in the *Angling Times* would ever have done.

So before you advertise, weigh up the costs against the number of useful targets you will reach, and make sure that this is the most cost-effective way in which to communicate with them. Remember that it doesn't matter whether your ad is seen by one person who will never buy from you or by fifty million. The only thing that matters is how many people see it who *might* buy from you.

Who are your customers?

The next question, then, is who might buy from you? Who are your potential customers? It's a fairly safe bet that many of them are the same as your existing customers. But there may also be other groups that you don't sell to at the moment but who might well buy from you if you let them know you're there (like the GP fishing enthusiasts staying at the hotel). So the first thing you need to do is to draw up a profile of your existing customers and your prospects.

At the end of Chapter 6 we dealt with keeping customer records. This is yet another one of those times they will prove invaluable. If you're selling to businesses, they should tell you whether your customers tend to be in service, retail or manufacturing businesses, large or small companies, and so on. Are the buyers usually specialist buyers, marketing directors, technical managers or who? If you're selling to the public, your records should indicate whether your customers are affluent or not, whether the majority of them are male or female, whereabouts they tend to live (city, town or village). If they are all local, they may well be concentrated in certain geographical areas – parts of town that are populated by retired people, or first-time buyers or whatever.

If you have been recording useful comments that your customers make, these may give you ideas for new groups of people to approach. For example, if you are a stationery supplier, you may have had a couple of customers mention that they are buying your top-of-the-range fountain pens for someone else. This might give you the idea of advertising them in October and November as ideal Christmas gifts.

EXERCISE

Suppose you're an accountant. What target customer groups do you think you might have? In the space below, write down about six ideas for groups you feel you should try to reach.

You may well have come up with all sorts of ideas that I haven't thought of, but here are a few suggestions that should show you whether you were thinking on the right lines.

- anyone who is running a small business (that has to be top of the list, really)
- professionals: doctors, dentists, architects, lawyers and so on
- anyone who is about to start up a small business
- people who are taking out mortgages
- people who have more than one source of income:
  - two-income families
  - people who run a second business (such as bed and breakfast)
  - people who let property to supplement their income (such as renting out the house they inherited, instead of selling it)
- People whose income has recently increased:
  - those who have been promoted
  - those who have received compensation payments, legacies or golden handshakes, or have just won the lottery
- People who find their accounts too complicated or stressful to do themselves:
  - people who have several pension, life insurance schemes and so on
  - the recently retired or bereaved

Advertising to these groups may well be an inexpensive way of finding out which of them really is as promising as you think. Once the ads have answered that question, you may advertise again, or you may decide to approach the responsive groups in some other way next time – by writing, or phoning, or exhibiting. Or perhaps by advertising to the same group but through a different advertising medium. So the next question is: what's the best way to reach these people?

—— How can you reach them? ——

You'll need to brainstorm the answer to this question. And pretend you're a customer (or a potential customer). For each target group, you need to ask yourself as many questions as you can until you have a clear idea of how to reach them. For example:

- What else do these people have in common (other than owning a small business, running a bed and breakfast, or whatever)? Are they all wealthy? Or retired? Or members of a conservation charity?

- Is there anywhere they tend to go? Football matches? A particular trade exhibition? Where do they shop?
- What do they tend to do with their spare time? Read? Go to the gym? Eat out?
- What sort of newspapers or magazines do they read? The local press? Trade publications? The parish newsletter? The local glossy magazine? The Federation of Small Businesses magazine?
- Which sections of the paper do they read? The horoscopes? The business page? The health and fitness section?
- What other businesses do they buy from? Estate agents? Fitness clubs? Lawn mower suppliers?

All of these questions – and endless others – can lead you to clues about how to reach high concentrations of target customers. If you sell tough waterproof clothing, for example, and you want to target walkers and ramblers, you could advertise in the newsletter of your local conservation organisation (conservationists also tend to be keen walkers). This may well cost less than advertising in the paper, and it goes straight to the people you most want to communicate with.

As an accountant, you could do worse than advertise through the customer newsletters of letting agents, solicitors, and insurance, pensions and financial advisors. You could ask to leave a few brochures in the local estate agents, banks and enterprise agencies. You could scour the business pages of the local paper and write (rather than advertise) to people who have recently been promoted. Your local tourist board will be in communication with owners of bed and breakfasts and holiday homes. They may send them a newsletter, or they may let you insert a leaflet in with their mailing. You could contact retired people, or those who are widowed and finding it hard to deal with the accounts, through local hairdressers, local clubs for retired people, or your local library, or wherever else you have found that they congregate.

Making the most of media advertising

Now that you know who your customers are, and how you can reach them, it's time to look at some of the options more closely. I'm assuming that you can't afford to advertise in the national papers, or on television. If by any chance I'm wrong, congratulations. The guidelines for advertising in the national press are exactly the same as for the local press, really; it just costs a lot more. If you are thinking of advertising on television, contact your local commercial station and ask their advice on where to find a good, reputable production company.

Which medium?

There are plenty of different places you could advertise. The costs vary and the accuracy of the targeting varies; you will need to establish both of these before you can decide where you are going to advertise. You can, of course, advertise in more than one place if you want to reach more than one group, or if you want to make more of an impression on your target group.

The local press

This can include dailies, weeklies, freesheets, parish magazines and so on. There is a tendency to assume that if your customers are local, and will therefore most probably read the local paper, you should advertise there in order to reach them. This is not necessarily the case, as we have just seen. If your target customers make up only a small percentage of the local populace, there are probably more cost-effective ways to reach them. If you want to communicate with them through the local press, do it for free with a press release – it's more than twice as likely to be read as well.

The businesses that should be using the local press are the ones whose target customers are just about everybody. People selling second-hand washing machines, or announcing the opening of a new discount carpet store. The key, once again, is to pretend you're a customer. If you wanted to buy a second-hand washing machine, where would you look? Probably in the local paper. Or – as in the case of the carpet store – if you didn't know you wanted to buy the product, would this information grab your attention? If you were advertising combine harvesters, probably not. Most people will never buy them, and those that do, know where to go for them. But the carpet store falls into a different category. Most people buy carpet at some time, and may well think 'I'll remember to have a look at that new place when I finally get round to recarpeting the hall.'

The local free newspapers are cheaper to advertise in than the paid-for ones. However, don't assume that everyone whose letterbox they fall through will read them. Many people chuck them straight in the bin. Likewise, the freesheets that carry advertising only, that are delivered to the door, are often not read. On the other hand, advertising-only papers that you have to pick up at the newsagents, or that you have to pay for, are well read – everybody who gets a copy wants to look at the ads.

The advertising sales staff at the local press will tell you that you are better off placing an ad for several issues in a row. You may think they are just saying this to persuade you to spend more money with them, but in fact research indicates that this is absolutely true. The dripping tap effect is important in advertising, unless you're selling a one-off item such as an old washing machine.

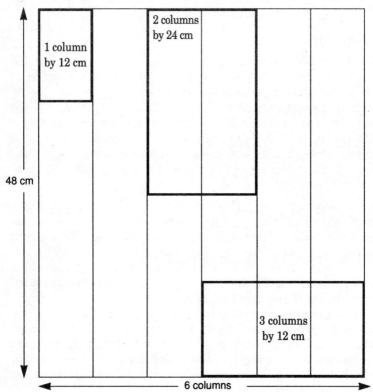

Should you use classified or display advertising? Classified ads have three or four lines of print, and are grouped under headings – display ads are designed, with headlines and maybe even illustrations, and can be anything up to a full page in size. Once again, where will your customers look for your product or service? You'd probably scan the classifieds if you were looking for second-hand furniture, but not if you wanted an accountant. Advertise wherever your target customers would look for your product.

Classified ads are cheaper, and you dictate the message over the phone. Display ads are sold in column widths and centimetre heights. So you can buy two columns by 10 cm, or one column by 8 cm.

Your best bet for information on the local press is to look them up in *BRAD Directory* at your nearest main library. It will tell you where to contact them and how much they charge. You can of course get the contact details from a copy of the paper. The advantage of using *BRAD* is that you will find out if there are any local papers – perhaps in neighbouring towns or areas – that you didn't know about and which might be useful.

Local magazines

The same guidelines apply for advertising in local magazines. They do tend to be more targeted, however. The question is whether their target reader matches your target customer. Again, look them up in *BRAD* to see what is around. There may be local business magazines, tourist magazines, home interest magazines and many more.

If you're not sure whether anyone actually reads these publications (and you do sometimes wonder), ask for a back copy and then ring a few of the advertisers and ask them if they got a response.

The trade press and specialist magazines

Once again, this is similar in principle to any other press advertising. And again, *BRAD* probably lists several trade publications in your target industry or market that you've never heard of. You may find this is more expensive than local press advertising, but remember that it may be far better targeted. If you cost it out, in terms of cost per target reached, it can work out far more cost effectively.

This may well be the best way to reach some of those specific groups of people you identified as targets. For example, you may decide to advertise your high-security filing cabinets to personnel managers, who hold a lot of confidential information on their employees. So perhaps you should place an ad in one of the personnel magazines. Or perhaps you have discovered that a high proportion of nature lovers are keen photographers; maybe you should advertise your specialist photographic equipment in a nature magazine.

Local radio

Radio ads are sold in time slots; your local station will give you details of costs and how to put the ad together. Ask them how many people they reach and what their listener profile is. As a general rule, local radio listeners are more likely to be women, they tend to be young or middle-aged, and probably downmarket. If this is your target audience, local radio advertising could be for you. It is usually better suited to 'news' advertising than regular 'awareness' advertising. In other words, use it to announce a sale, a new opening or a special event, rather than for generalised 'we're still here' advertising.

The local cinema

You buy cinema advertising in time slots, usually of 20, 30, 40 or 60 seconds. The production costs can be high, so use this medium only if you are aiming at a similar profile to cinema-goers. This isn't easy, since you don't know when you book the ad which films it will appear alongside, but as a general guide, movie-goers are likely to be under 25.

This can be a useful way to promote a locally available product or service – places to eat after the film are popularly advertised in the cinema. If your budget is tight, don't try to be clever with it. Keep it simple and smart, rather than fussy and cheap-looking. It's better to go for a voice-over with a couple of high quality still photographs than for cheaply put together moving pictures. Your local cinema can give you details of the costs and will recommend local production companies.

Business phone directories

You should always use your free, single line entry in *Yellow Pages* or *The Thomson Directory*. Past customers may use it to look up your name if they've forgotten it. But should you pay for a display ad? To answer that, you have to pretend you're a customer, once again. If a customer wants to buy whatever it is you sell, will they use the directory to find a supplier? If you're a 24-hour plumber, almost certainly yes. So your ad should be big and eye-catching, to compete with all the other 24-hour plumbers in there.

But how many people use a directory to find an accountant? Probably very few; they want a recommendation from a friend or another reputable business, or at least an ad in a respectable publication. People are worried about being ripped off by accountants, so they tend to look for recommendations from sources they feel they can trust.

Poster sites

Posters can be a good way to keep reminding everyone that you're there. They are a useful medium only if you are targeting the general public, and they should be designed to be read fast: often by people who are driving past at 40 or 50 mph. You normally buy poster space in multiples of a month, and it is better for long term 'awareness' advertising than for 'news' advertising.

BRAD carries listings of poster site contractors; don't forget to allow for the cost of designing and printing the posters, which will be greater than the cost of producing a newspaper or magazine ad.

On the buses

The ads inside buses can be inexpensive, but the ads on the outside will be seen by more people. The guidelines for advertising on the outside of buses are similar to those for poster advertising. But since the bus moves, it takes the poster to the people. Bus companies reckon that after about a month, over three quarters of the people in your area will have seen your ad. The longer it stays up, the more often they will see it. Bus advertising is listed in *BRAD*.

It's a good idea to check the route of the buses your posters are going on. In theory, the bus could change routes, but it isn't likely to. If you want to advertise something people can buy at the shops, advertise on a bus that goes through the shopping centre. If you advertise inside the bus, advertise something that the people in the bus will pass close to on their journey.

If you want to advertise inside the bus, remember that you are advertising to people who travel by bus: they are more likely to be elderly, probably low-income, and they probably don't have cars. So it may not be the ideal place to promote your riding stable that is five miles from the nearest bus stop or train station.

Brochures and leaflets

These can be put through letterboxes, stuck on car windscreens, left in other businesses' premises or handed out on the street. Or inserted into newspapers and magazines. Letterbox distribution is relatively cheap: you can do it yourself or pay your local newspaper to do it.

You can't target this kind of advertising accurately, although you can restrict your leaflet drops to houses in the smarter parts of town, or leave your leaflet only on BMWs and Mercedes.

If you're distributing door to door, forget businesses unless you are targeting receptionists. The brochure won't get any further than that without a name on it (if you have a name, it's more sensible to post it).

You could display your brochures in a complementary business. If you run a bakery, why not ask to display your brochures for wedding cakes in the local wedding outfitters? Why not suggest that you also distribute each other's leaflets or brochures? A local plumber and a local tiler could both benefit from handing each other's leaflets out to customers.

Inserts in newspapers and magazines are more expensive than ads. On the other hand, they can get you five times the response that a full page ad can.

DIY adverts

It's far cheaper to write and design your own ad than to pay someone else to do it. You may still need to pay a designer to put it all together in a form that a printer or a newspaper can use. You will also need a designer, most probably, if you sell high-quality products through high-quality magazines. But even if you can afford to pay someone else, you should still understand the basics of writing and designing ads yourself. Otherwise, how will you know you're getting your money's worth from the agency or designer you are using?

Writing your ad

Another book in this series, *Teach Yourself Copywriting*, will tell you all you need to know about writing your ad. But I will give you a guide to the important points. There's a very useful mnemonic to help you write advertising copy: AIDA. It stands for a four-stage process:

- Attention
- Interest
- Desire
- Action

These are the four ingredients that all good ads should have. Let's look at each one in turn.

Attention

The first thing the reader will look at is the photograph (if there is one). If, and only if, that grabs their attention, they will read the headline. That's probably as far as they get; within 1½ seconds most readers give up and move on. Your job is to grab their attention in those 1½ seconds, and keep them reading.

You can do this with the photograph (I'll deal with photographs a little later on) and the headline. The most important thing about a headline is that it should sell a benefit (we looked at benefits in Chapter 6). The headline's job is to answer the reader's question: 'What's in it for me?' before they have even thought to ask it. And with less than two seconds before the reader moves on, you only have time to mention one benefit.

So what benefit should you emphasise? Well, what is your product or service's unique selling proposition, or USP? A USP is the thing that makes your product different from everyone else's: it's the cheapest, or the after-sales service is better, or it's better quality or whatever. Sometimes the USP is comparative; in other words your product may not be the best quality available but it may be the best quality for the price it is.

You must establish what your product's USP is. I know a dentist who specialises in being good with kids. That's his USP and he capitalises on it. He keeps plenty of toys in the waiting room, sticks fun posters up on his ceiling above the chair, and tells the kids jokes. It sets him apart from other dentists.

So decide what your USP is and, unless this is a one-off ad to promote a special event, use it in your headline. The other time you might vary it is if you're targeting a new audience: perhaps your business customers are more interested in your fast delivery than your domestic customers, who are more tempted by your prices. In this case you have two USPs, one for each clearly-defined target group.

So pick a headline that offers a benefit, and that benefit is your USP. As an accountant promoting your services to elderly people who find it hard to cope with their accounts, you could say: *If you don't enjoy managing your own finances, there's an easy alternative.* There's a clear benefit there.

There are a few additional points about headlines to bear in mind:

- Including the price in the headline makes the ad more memorable. (However, this is useful only if price is important to your customers.)
- The more specific you are, the better. Don't say *This will save money on your fuel bills*, say *This will save at least 20 per cent on your fuel bills*.
- Headlines with between ten and seventeen words are most likely to be read (but not if you have to cram a long headline into a small space – in this case, settle for a shorter headline).

There are certain words that people are attracted to or put off by, and it's a good idea to know which they are. The experts sometimes know how to get away with using 'negative' words in a headline, but the likes of us shouldn't mess with them. (Even the experts misjudge it occasionally). So here is a list of words that attract readers, and a list of words to avoid in your headlines.

Positive words		Negative words	
new	you	death	buy
introducing	special offer	risk	order
free	bargain	worry	cost
announcing	discount	wrong	pay
unique	money off	difficult	contract
alternative	save	problem	tax
easy	limited time only	bad	bill
comfortable	sale	accident	decision
love	guarantee	fail	commitment
benefits	discover	loss	obligation
results	secret		

EXERCISE

You're on your own now. I can't give you any answers to this exercise because I don't know your business. But you should find that you learn a lot simply from doing it. Decide (if you don't already know) what your USP is, and then devise three different headlines that express it as a benefit to the reader. Try to include at least one word from the 'positive words' list above in each headline, and avoid using the 'negative words'.

USP

Headline 1

Headline 2

Headline 3

The last place the reader will look before they decide whether to read the ad or not, is the bottom right hand corner. This is where they expect to find out who you are. So put your company name there, clearly.

Interest

Now you've got their attention. At the end of your initial 1½ seconds, the readers are still with you. The next thing to do is to turn that attention into genuine interest. Make them want to read all about it.

We're a selfish bunch, really. We like hearing and reading about ourselves. So keep telling your readers what this product or service can do for them. Many advertisers have a tendency, once they are past the headline, to go back to talking about features. But that's not the way to hold the readers' interest.

Don't start by repeating what you've already said in the headline. Tell them something that will genuinely interest them. You could do this by asking a question ('how long does it take you to fill in your tax return every year?'), or telling them something they didn't know before ('63 per cent of people spend more than two hours a month sorting out their finances'). Any information you quote of this sort should, of course, be accurate. You could use humour to catch their interest, but make sure it's genuinely funny. There's nothing worse than humour which fails.

Follow through the ad, however long or short, by telling your readers what your product or service can do for them. If you have room, use sub-headings. They are the next thing readers will look at once you've got their attention. But, of course, they must hold the reader's interest by focusing on the benefits. So your sub-headings should not say 'Tax returns' but 'You can forget about tax returns'.

Anything in quotes will help to hold the readers' interest. Get one of your customers to endorse the product or service, and then quote them in the ad. The simplest way to do it is to write the testimonial yourself and then ask the customer to put their name to it. Tell them you've drafted the words to save them the trouble.

There are various techniques you can use in your writing style to keep the reader hooked:

- Write in the second person – address the reader as you. Don't say 'this product saves time' say 'this product will save you time'.
- Use linking phrases to move smoothly from one sentence or paragraph to the next: 'That's because...' 'After all...' 'And there's more...' 'Not only...' 'And of course...' and so on.
- Repeat certain words or phrases: 'You can forget your tax return, you can forget the inland revenue...'
- Keep your language simple and clear, using short words and short sentences.

Desire

The reader is interested in the product. But does he or she actually want to buy it? That's the next crucial ingredient in your ad. It doesn't follow the interest, it runs alongside it. As you have been writing the ad, you should have been cultivating a desire in your readers to own your product or take advantage of your service. All those benefits you've been writing about should achieve this.

But people often give themselves excuses not to buy things. They tell themselves 'I probably can't afford it' or 'I'll still have to do most of my accounts myself' or 'I don't want my financial affairs to be common knowledge.' So as the text of the ad progresses, the balance should shift from explaining the benefits to reassuring the reader: *Most of our customers find that our fee is more than covered by the money we can save them... You can hand over as much or as little of your finances as you choose... Your financial affairs will remain completely private. We'll sign a confidentiality agreement to guarantee it.*

You should know from your research (in Chapter 2), and from the questions you are most often asked, what people's main reservations are. So make sure you address them. In a conversation, you can tell when someone sounds concerned and you can put their mind at rest. When you advertise, you have to address every concern before the readers ever makes contact. If you don't, they won't get in touch and you'll never know who they were.

Action

If you look through your local paper, you may be surprised to notice how many advertisers miss this stage out. This is the crucial bit where you tell the reader what to do now that you've persuaded them they want the product. They can:

- Return the coupon. This tends to get a good response. If you use a coupon, make sure your ad is positioned at the corner of a page where it is easy for the reader to cut or tear it out. It can often make the difference between whether they bother or not. And try to ensure that the back of the page isn't something people will want to save, such as a recipe or a checklist of some kind, or next Saturday's television listing. You need people to cut the coupon now before they forget;
- Cut out the coupon and use it to get a discount. This way, they don't even have to bother to fill it in;
- Phone you. It's friendlier if you can give them a name to ask for; this is much easier for you than it is for a larger company. After the ad comes out, make sure you are going to be around to answer the phone. If you're away exhibiting that week, for example, hold the ad until you get back;
- Go down to the shops and buy your product;
- Call in and visit your shop, showroom or office;
- Pick up a brochure. Tell them where from – their local library, your offices or wherever.

The easier you make it, the more likely they are to do it. The kind of advertising where you ask readers to contact you (by phone, fax, e-mail or post) is called direct response advertising. You're asking them to communicate with you directly as a result of the ad, rather than go to their local shop to buy your product, or bear you in mind when they finally get round to recarpeting the hall. Direct response advertising is part of what is known as direct marketing, which is what Chapter 9 is about. It is particularly useful for small businesses, because the chances are that you can't afford to invest much money in advertising unless you're going to get orders back in as a direct result. Long term awareness advertising (such as *Go to work on an egg*) usually has to be for the larger companies – you just want to get those cheques rolling in.

It's worth just mentioning that if you place an ad for goods in the United Kingdom in which you ask for money before the goods are delivered, you must register with the Mail Order Protection Scheme if the ad is going in the national press, or with equivalent organisations for other newspapers and magazines. The Mail Order Protection Scheme (see 'Useful Addresses') can give you information about this.

Designing your ad

Now you know what you're going to say, what should it look like? Here are a few guidelines:

- Always print text against a white or pale background – it's far easier to read;
- An uncluttered ad with plenty of 'white space' around the text and illustrations will attract the reader's eye;
- Don't print text in capitals; it's much harder to read;
- Remember your company image and identity, and make sure you follow it through in your advertising;
- Use illustrations or photos if you can, but remember that they won't work if you can't afford a big enough space to show them off well. And the reproduction quality, especially in newspapers, can be poor: small photos will often come out as nothing but a smudgy blur;
- Consider what your competitors' ads look like. If they all pay for a half-page full colour ad, you may have to do the same or your business is likely to appear small and cheap. You may be able to make a virtue of this ('we keep our prices low because we don't waste money on advertising' sort of thing), but it doesn't always work. It

has to be a headline, for a start, or the readers will never get to it. And that means that you've wasted your headline on something that is not necessarily your best benefit;

● Look at other people's ads whenever you read a paper or walk past a poster. Judge for yourself what is attention-grabbing, what looks cheap or expensive, what is elegant or clumsy and so on. Learn from other people's mistakes – it saves the expense of making your own. And learn from their good achievements as well.

Using photographs and illustrations

The function of the photograph or illustration is to attract people's attention. It must be relevant, and it must relate to the headline in some way (which is the next thing they will look at). You don't have to say everything there is to say with the illustration. Indeed you would confuse the reader if you tried. This is not the place to impart every tiny benefit of the product. The function of the illustration is to persuade the reader to look at the rest of the ad. That's it.

Photographs are usually better than drawings – people tend to believe them – but a 5 cm square photograph in smudgy newsprint isn't going to sell anything. A bad photograph is worse than no photo at all. Assuming you have room for one, however, the best kind of photograph is one that shows your product in action. Before and after photos can also work well.

After the headline, the readers (if they are still interested) will go back and read the caption, if there is one. They should be able to understand the photo without reading the caption, however. If they didn't *understand* it by the time they had read the headline, they probably never got as far as the caption. So the function of the caption is not to explain the photograph. However, you won't want to waste space by repeating the information in the headline. So use the caption to emphasise an additional point, for example: *It takes as little two minutes to erect the Metrocamp tent* under a photo of the tent. This should encourage people to read on and find out more.

If you can, include people in your photograph, preferably using the product. This has all sorts of advantages:

● It helps to give the photograph movement and action;
● It gives the reader something to identify with ('Ah! people' they think – unconsciously – 'I'm one of them. This is obviously my type of product.')

- It can be useful for adding a visual scale to the product (it tells you whether the wardrobe you're advertising is 150 cm or 250 cm high)
- If you are selling a service and not a product, it's usually the best way to illustrate it. You can show someone enjoying their holiday, or putting their feet up because you're looking after the kids for them.

If you don't enjoy managing your finances, there's an easy alternative

You're not alone. In fact, 90 per cent of people would prefer to hand the job over to someone else.

And now you can. No more struggling with figures. No more wasted time filling in your tax return. No more dealing with the Inland Revenue.

What's more, you could find it saves you more money than it costs you. Many of our clients do.

You can hand over as much or as little of your finances as you choose. And your financial affairs will remain completely private. We'll sign a confidentiality agreement to guarantee it.

If you'd like more information, in confidence, call John Brown or Mary Smith now on 01234–567890 and ask for a brochure on how to take the stress out of managing your money.

PSA Accountancy Services
25 High Street, Bakerstown AB1 2CD

Before going on to look at the techniques for measuring how effective your advertising has been, let's just take a look at an example of one of the simplest kinds of ad, the type that small businesses use most frequently: a black and white display ad with no room for a photograph. The kind of thing you can put together inexpensively for leaflets, local magazines, local papers and the trade press. This should give you an idea of what ordinary people like you and me can do with a small space, and no professional copywriter or designer. It should follow rule four of marketing a small business: don't try to be too perfect.

Did it work?

First of all, did it happen? Make sure that all the ads you book and pay for do actually appear where and when they are supposed to. Get yourself one of those big cuttings books, and stick into it a copy of every ad you produce. Write the date and publication by each one, and make a note of where it appeared (which page, and opposite or near to what type of editorial).

If you include a return coupon in your ad, you'll know how many people respond. If you place the ad more than once, make each one fractionally different, or print a small code number in the bottom left hand corner. That way, you'll know which publication and which issue each coupon comes from. Even the same ad in the same paper on consecutive days should be coded; you may find that more people respond on a Friday than a Tuesday. You will, of course, record these responses in your customer records which we covered in Chapter 6. Then you can easily measure the cost of the ad against the value of the orders and new leads that it generated.

But what if you weren't asking for a direct response to your ad? When someone rings up out of the blue and asks for a brochure or places an order, how do you know where they heard of you? Was it the ad in the local paper or the poster on the bus? Or was it a leaflet on their car windscreen? It might not have been an ad at all. It could have been a mailshot you sent out, or an exhibition, or word of mouth.

The way to find out is simple: ask them. 'May I ask where you heard of us?' Then note it down on their records. And when I say all new enquiries, I mean all. If you forget to ask them, phone them back and ask – they never seem to mind. After a while you'll start to get a picture: more people respond in the summer than the winter, perhaps. Or lots of people respond to the ads in the county magazine, for example, but very few people mention the ad in the local cinema. It should be fairly clear which of those ads is most worth repeating.

There's a reason why you must note on each prospect's records where they heard of you (rather than keep a list that isn't cross-referenced with individual contacts). You may find, for example, that the majority of people get your name from the *Yellow Pages*, but that most of the people who actually place orders got your name from the ad in the local glossy magazine. Enquiries and orders aren't the same thing.

As well as enabling you to judge the effectiveness of your advertising, this information also gives you a fuller picture of who your target customers are – the kind of people who read the county magazine, say, or the type of people who go to the cinema. All of this information can be fed into the system to guide your PR (perhaps your press releases need to be in the county magazine more than in the local weekly paper), to target your mailshots better, to help you decide which are the best exhibitions to attend and so on. As we've already seen, you need to have as clear a picture as possible of who your customers and potential customers are. And it becomes more crucial than ever when you start to communicate with them by mail, as we'll see in Chapter 9.

9

DIRECT MARKETING

Direct marketing is one of those modern buzz phrases that everyone bandies about, despite the fact that, secretly, a lot of them are unsure of exactly what it means. The reason I have succumbed to using it is because, once you understand what it is, it's the best way to describe it.

Direct marketing is any form of selling in which you communicate *directly* with the customer, and elicit some kind of response. So it doesn't cover selling through retailers, distributors or wholesalers, and it doesn't cover any advertising that doesn't ask the reader for a response (as we saw in Chapter 8). What it does cover is:

- direct mail
- mail order
- telemarketing
- direct response advertising (which we covered in Chapter 8)
- face-to-face selling (which we looked at in Chapter 6)

This chapter will concentrate on the first three areas.

—— Benefits of direct marketing ——

It's fairly clear that direct marketing, at least in some of its forms, has been around for quite a while. People have been writing to customers for centuries, and selling to them face to face for thousands of years. But over the last few years businesses have started to realise the huge potential of this form of marketing, and have honed and fine-tuned the techniques to make direct marketing more profitable than ever before.

The point about direct marketing is that you are in communication with all your customers on an individual level. That means that you can find out far more about them than you could if they bought your products from a retailer. You know which of your customers tend to buy at Christmas time, which ones spend a lot of money with you and which spend a little, which will order when you contact them and which place a regular order once a month, whether you call them or not.

And, as you will realise, that means that you can target your marketing far more accurately. You don't have to phone or mail every customer with every catalogue, offer, invitation or whatever. You can save time and money by making certain offers only to the customers who have taken advantage of that kind of offer in the past. You can test new products on the customers who have bought related products in the past. You can send a catalogue of your more expensive items only to people who have tended to buy the more expensive items in the past, and so on. This has two key benefits:

1 It saves you money in terms of time, printing bills, phone bills, administration costs and so on;
2 It enables you to address each customer in a more personal way, which you can use to increase the likelihood of their buying from you and which, as we saw in Chapter 5, helps to increase their loyalty to your company. For example, you can send them a letter saying 'We hope you are enjoying the sun lounger you bought from us earlier this year. You might be interested to know that we have just introduced a range of garden parasols...'

Your database

Ideally, you will want a sophisticated database to store all this information. Not only will you want to keep a lot of details on record (as we saw in Chapter 6), but you also want to be able to cross-reference them. For example, you might send invitations to visit your exhibition stand in Bristol to all the people who are based in south-west England. But you could also divide these people into those who have ordered from you in the last year and those who haven't. Then you can mail two separate letters, making each one more personalised than if you had sent the same letter to all your customers in the area.

As I said, you will *want* a sophisticated database. But you may not be able to afford one. Don't worry – it's perfectly possible to do this with a manual card index file (and if your next mailing goes out when there's a power cut, you'll feel really smug). It takes a little longer, but it can be done and it's well worthwhile. And you can comfort yourself with the thought that it's one of the most effective ways to make enough money to invest in a sophisticated computerised database.

Building a mailing list

We have already looked at a lot of the ways of building a mailing list. The most useful names and addresses are those of people who have bought from you in the past. After that, the next most useful are the contact details of people who have made enquiries but not yet placed an order. But where do you find the rest of your contacts?

First, you will keep building on both the lists you already have. People from your 'enquiries only' list will begin to swell your 'people who have ordered' list. And your 'enquiries only' list will increase, especially if your advertising brings in requests for appointments, phone calls or brochures. And of course you'll have the details of anyone who has ever visited your exhibition stand.

But you can also acquire lists from other people, by buying or renting them, or even by acquiring them for free. You already know who your target customers are – we covered that at the beginning of Chapter 8. Now you want to get hold of their names and addresses. Names are very important. If you possibly can, phone or write to people by name. It is far more personal – and we've already seen the benefits of that – and it's far more likely to get through to them. It's worth paying extra to get a list with contact names. If you have a business list without names, the chances of your mailshots getting through are minimal (unless you're mailing the receptionist). Even putting 'The Buyer' or 'The Chief Engineer' on the envelope won't help much. The thing to do is to phone and ask for the names and add them to your database before you mail out. If there are too many to do this, the only advice I can give you is don't use the list at all. It will be more cost effective in the long run to pay more for a list that comes with contact names.

Buying lists

Your local main library should have a copy of *BRAD Direct Marketing*, which brings out a directory of available mailing lists which is updated every six months. They should also have a copy of the quarterly publication *Lists and Data Sources*. In addition to this, the Direct Marketing Association (or DMA, see 'Useful Addresses') has a listing of mailing list brokers. Some associations and professional institutions will sell you lists of their members, or sections of their members (such as all those in Scotland).

The cost of buying a list varies considerably, but you should be able to assess whether they are worth it. What is your usual response rate? Work out the likely number of responses, and from this calculate their total value. Then measure this against the cost of buying the list.

There are several things to check before you pay for a list:

- Find out how the list was compiled. Suppose you sell high-quality children's garden equipment (slides and sand pits, and so on). Is this a list of families with children under 12, and an income of at least £40 000, who subscribe to *Country Living*? Or are they simply families with pre-teenage children? It makes a difference to how much the list is worth to you. You want it to match the profile of your prospects as closely as possible. Also, it's worth knowing that most people either will or won't buy through the post. If they are among the many who just won't, you're wasting your money mailing them. So it helps to buy a list which has been filtered to include only people who have bought through the post in the past;
- Is it accurate and up to date? You don't want to pay for 5000 names only to find that 1000 of them have changed their address since the list was compiled. Or perhaps some names have ended up on the list twice (or even more), as lists have been merged;
- In what form will you receive the list? If you have a computer, make sure you get the list on a compatible disk. If you don't have a computer, make sure you can get the list printed out;
- Ask to test a sample, and find out what size you can test. If you want to mail 50 000 people, you want to know before you pay for

the names that you are using a suitable list. The minimum sample size is generally 5000, although you may be able to negotiate a smaller 'first time buyer' deal. Bear in mind, though, that the average response rate to an unsolicited mailshot to non-customers is between 1 and 2 per cent. So you need to mail a fair number to get a clear idea of the usefulness of the list. 5000 names would get you an expected response of only 25 to 50. A smaller sample would barely be statistically reliable.

Renting lists

This is obviously a little cheaper than buying a list. You can reckon to spend broadly in the region of £150 per thousand names. You can rent lists from many trade and professional institutions and associations, and also from the *Yellow Pages*, who can break down their mailing list into individual post code districts, and divide them into around two thousand categories.

Don't attempt to use a rental list more often than you have paid to. They tend to include a few built-in names to check on your mailings, so you're likely to get caught. You will need to make the same checks as I listed above for bought lists, and a few others as well:

- Ask to see the address labels. Make sure they would make the recipient want to open the envelope. If they are printed in capital letters on a dot matrix printer they are not going to get as good a response rate as if they look neatly typed;
- Find out what response rate the list has elicited in the past. Of course, you will need to take into account the nature of the mailing, but it gives you a reasonable idea of how good the list is. Check at the same time what price bracket the goods advertised in past mailings were; this will affect the response rate.

Free lists

You can create your own lists from the various sources of ready-made information we looked at in Chapter 2 – directories, yearbooks, and so on. If you need huge numbers of customers in order to make a profit this may not be feasible, but if you sell relatively few items at a high profit you could use this approach. Try mailing, say, fifty or a hundred of these contacts and see how many respond, and which ones. This should help you select the next fifty or a hundred names more effectively.

Along the same lines, you can often pick up useful leads by trawling the press – especially if you sell to businesses. Keep the details of companies who have had successes or who are advertising for staff.

Another source of free mailing lists is those belonging to other companies. The obvious way to get hold of these is to swap them for your own list, although you're free to do any deal you like. If you sell computer stationery, maybe the local computer hardware supplier will give you their mailing list in exchange for a year's free supply of computer listing paper.

The important thing is to approach a business that has a different product or service but very similar customers to you. You may not get much joy from your direct competitors, but there should be other companies around that can gain as much from you as you can from them. The two computer supply companies I just mentioned are a good example.

Another, excellent option is to ask your customers for referrals. We've already examined this in Chapter 6, and it's a good way to build up a mailing list that should get a good response rate.

Looking after your mailing list

Mailing lists can go out of date frighteningly fast. Make sure yours stays 'clean'. The two key exercises are known as merging and purging.

Merging You may have the same person listed twice, for all sorts of reasons. He or she may have made an enquiry twice and been listed both times, or they may have been on both your own list and another that you bought. So you need to merge duplications. For business contacts, by the way, it's a good idea to mail each contact in the company separately. So merge the same contact name if it's listed twice, but don't merge everyone in the company into one mailing.

Purging This involves cleaning out all the old and out-of-date names of people who have moved away. You will also, sooner or later, want to purge the names of people who have been on your list for more than a certain length of time without buying anything. The time will vary according to your product – business customers will buy stationery more often than domestic customers buy climbing frames for their children. But you will learn, from studying your customer records, when it becomes more cost-effective to give up on a customer than to keep mailing them. You can always send out one final mailing saying 'please return this reply-paid card if you would like to stay on our mailing list.'

There are two simple ways you can clean your list. One is to send out a card to each customer once a year, with a mailing you were sending anyway, asking them to let you know if any of their details have changed. Make it easy for them: give them a Freepost or reply-paid card to return, with your address on one side and their address label on the other, asking them to mark any corrections on it. The easier this process is for them, the more likely they are to bother. You should do this quite regularly so that your letter reaches anyone who *has* moved before they stop getting their post forwarded.

The other way to clean your list is to put a return address on the envelope. This has two disadvantages, however. One is that it can put people off opening the letter because it looks like a mailshot (which it is), and the other is that you will have to pay for first class postage or the Royal Mail can't guarantee to return the undelivered letters. Again, you could do this once a year as a clean-up operation; the extra postage costs should be offset by the money you save from not having to mail all the out-of-date addresses in future. If you're unsure about it, try using a return address and first-class postage for half your mailing only. Compare the response rates and the number of returns, and calculate whether it's worth it.

If you have a fairly short mailing list, you could phone round once every year or two to check whether anyone's details have changed.

Direct mail

The first thing to do with direct mail, as with everything else, is to set an objective. To do that, you need to decide what you are trying to achieve by writing to these customers or prospects. Do you want them to send back an order and a cheque to go with it, or do you just want them to agree to an appointment? Direct mail can be useful for both of these, and anything in between, such as visiting your exhibition stand or phoning for more information.

Once you know what reaction you want, you can set your objective. If you are used to sending out mailshots, you will know what response rate to expect, what value order you are likely to get and so on. If this is your first mailshot, assume a modest estimate of a 2 per cent response rate for the purpose of costing (unless you know of some reason why this should be higher). Suppose 2 per cent of the people you mail agree to an appointment. You know from your records what proportion of your appointments you expect to convert into sales, so you should be able to estimate the profit you aim to make from the exercise.

The other thing you should consider before you start is how you will cope with the response. If you mail 10 000 people, you can reasonably expect to receive 200 replies. Can you manufacture, or afford to buy in, enough stock? Will you be able to deal with them on top of all your usual workload? Or can you lighten your usual workload?

If you think this will be a problem, your best bet (assuming you can't afford to take on extra staff to help) is to stagger your mailing. If you send out batches of 1000 a week, you should receive 20 replies a week; much easier to cope with.

Writing a direct mail letter

Remember the points about company image we covered in Chapter 3? It's a crucial factor in deciding what kind of letter to send people. If you have an individual relationship with your customers, they will expect a personalised letter. If your customers have never met you in the flesh and don't expect to, you can send a less personalised letter. Equally, people will expect a discreet sales approach from some companies and a fairly obvious one from others. I'll give you a couple of examples: an accountant approaching prospects to suggest taking over their financial affairs would be expected to adopt a soft sell approach. But you would expect a fairly hard sell from a discount carpet warehouse.

The hard-sell letter

If you're sending a hard sell type of letter, it's really an ad that you send through the post. The rules for writing this kind of letter are the same as for writing ads: AIDA (attention, interest, desire, action). After the name at the top of the page, you can even insert a headline before you continue the letter. The letter should be about a page long at the most if you're writing to a business contact – they won't have time to read more than that – but you can make it a little longer for home addresses. Don't, however, try to do those eight-page letters that the Reader's Digest send out; remember small business marketing rule five – know your limitations.

There are a few additional points to make about this kind of sales letter, in addition to the AIDA format that you already know from Chapter 8:

- You need to grab attention in order to compete with all the other letters that your prospects receive. (The average business person receives fourteen items of direct mail each week.) Send something with yours: a sample, a money-off voucher, a prize draw ticket;
- If you really can't personalise every letter as well as the envelopes, don't start 'Dear Sir/Madam' or 'Dear Customer'. Just start 'Good morning' or 'Hello';
- Take advantage of the additional space you have (compared with most advertisements) by including testimonials from your customers. We looked at how to solicit these in Chapter 8;
- If you possibly can, offer a no-quibble money-back guarantee;
- Don't grovel to the reader. Saying 'I humbly beg to remain your obedient servant...' or 'We would be honoured if you would favour us with your presence...' implies you are begging a favour. You're not. You're offering a mutually beneficial deal;
- Use a 'handwritten' PS at the end of the letter – it can double your response rate if it's well chosen. It should repeat something you've already said in the letter, which should give them a reason to respond promptly: 'Remember – the offer closes on 31 December' or 'We have limited stocks, so order now!'

The soft-sell letter

This should read like a letter from an acquaintance, and the selling needs to be approached much more gently. You can still use the AIDA format but pitch it discreetly. But you still need to address the readers as 'you', focus on the benefits to them, and all the other techniques that are a part of any kind of selling (as we saw in Chapter 6).

Dear Mrs MacDonald

How many generations has your kitchen table been in the family?

Most kitchen tables last between twenty and thirty years before they are replaced. But the best crafted tables last down the centuries. And the older they become, the more cherished they are. It's a fact we're very conscious of at Bakerstown Country Furniture.

We like to imagine our kitchen tables as they will be in a few hundred years time. And our dining tables, wardrobes, chests and four poster beds. Still as sturdy, reliable and attractive as ever, and giving your great-great-grandchildren as much pleasure as they give you.

Of course, as a customer of ours, you appreciate the time and skill that we put into our furniture. And you know that each piece is different. No one else's is quite like yours. This means, of course, that you have to see each individual piece to know what its unique qualities are.

And now you can. We will be opening a new showroom at 35 Bakersfield High Street at the end of the month. You will find two invitations enclosed with this letter. I would be delighted if you could join us for the opening on 28 March, where you can admire some of our most recent pieces of furniture over a glass of wine.

I'll be in touch in the next week or two to see if you'll be free to come along.

I look forward to speaking to you soon, and to welcoming you to our showroom.

With best wishes

Linda Brown

Linda Brown
Proprietor
Bakerstown Country Furniture

EXERCISE

It's time to try it for yourself. Imagine you sell upmarket, hand-crafted country furniture. You are writing to existing customers to invite them to the opening of your new shop, in Bakerstown High Street. If you don't know anything about furniture, make it up – it doesn't matter. Just concentrate on the style and format of the letter.

There are, of course, no right or wrong answers to this exercise. I'll give you a sample answer because you might find it helpful, but you could perfectly well have written an excellent letter that bears little relation to mine, so don't worry if there are a lot of differences.

It's often the case that if you're sending this kind of letter you have a relatively small customer database. That's why your relationship with your customers is individual. So you may be sending out quite small mailshots. If you are writing to business customers, you can attract their attention by faxing the letter. It doesn't seem like a hard sell approach because it actually draws attention to the fact that you know them personally.

You can still send free gifts and tickets with this kind of letter (obviously not if you fax it), but go for a sample rather than putting their name in a prize draw. If your mailing is small, try to leave the ball in your own court when it comes to the 'action' at the end of the letter. 'I'll give you a ring in the next few days to see if you can make it along to the product launch' – and then, of course, do what you say you will.

How to make sure they open it

Your letter could be competing with several others on the doormat. So here are a few tricks of the trade to help persuade the recipient to open it:

- Make sure the envelope suits the contents. If the letter is personalised, handwrite the envelopes if this is feasible. If you're selling an expensive, upmarket product, don't use cheap envelopes;
- It can help to trail the contents on the outside: 'Open now to find your prize draw number...' This gives away that the envelope contains a mailshot, of course (and one person's direct mail is someone else's junk mail). This may not matter; this is a good one to test on a small mailing and see how it affects your response rates. It is not a good idea for soft sell letters, as you would imagine, and it doesn't tend to work well for business prospects either;
- Hard sell letters should say so on the outside if there is a free gift inside;
- With hard sell letters, you could test different brightly coloured envelopes on a sample of your mailing list, as this can have a positive effect.

How to make sure they read it

Make sure that the letter itself is neatly printed, well laid out and follows through your corporate identity. Here are a few more tips to encourage people to read the letter:

- Remember from the last chapter how the reader's eye moves round the page. It's the same for a direct mail letter. Use charts, photographs or line drawings to illustrate the points you are making in the letter;
- For hard-sell letters, try printing in a second colour (if you can afford it – again, a test mailing will show you if it pays for itself in increased responses). Use the second colour for headlines, sub-headings and the PS, and to underline key phrases (just three or four to a page or you dilute the effect too much);
- If your letter is more than a page long, finish the page in mid-sentence, so they have to turn over to finish it. That way, they are more likely to keep on reading the next side;
- Keep the layout interesting with bullet points, sub-headings and so on;
- Indent the first line of each paragraph;
- Don't justify the right-hand margin (in other words, don't line up the right-hand ends of all the lines on the page).

How to make sure they reply

Assuming you are asking the reader to respond (which you will be unless *you* are going to contact *them*), you must make it as easy as possible for them. I have included tips about order forms a little further on under mail order; if you want people to order as a result of a direct mail letter rather than a catalogue, the same guidelines apply.

- Include a reply-paid envelope (for business customers you can get away without paying for the reply). Remember that you end up paying only for the ones that reply, and they should be worth the cost of the postage to you;
- Make sure the envelope is big enough to hold the order form;
- The envelope doesn't need to be expensive;
- If you want a response but not an order at this stage, send a reply-paid card asking them to tick boxes: please send me a brochure, please call to arrange an appointment, and so on.

Mail order

Many of the same rules apply to running a mail order business – or the mail-order arm of a business – as to sending out direct mail of other kinds. You still need to send a letter, although you can print this on the first page of the catalogue rather than sending it separately.

Collect as many mail order catalogues as you can. Get on their mailing lists and see what letters they send out, what offers they make, what their delivery times are and so on. And take a look at the kind of products they sell. A good mail order product should be unique, or too rare to be able to buy in the average high street (at least at the price). It should also be the kind of thing that people are happy to buy without seeing it, or without a demonstration.

As well as the points that apply from earlier in this chapter, here are the top ten rules for selling by mail order:

1 It can take several catalogues for people to start ordering from you, but once they have placed an order they are more likely to order again. Don't overestimate the value of the sales from your first mailing; expect a 1 per cent response at best and aim to break even. Only once you start to mail established customers can you expect to make a healthy profit – reckon on three years before you start to make money;

2 The accuracy of your targeting is never so important as in mail order. Your catalogues can easily cost £1 each to produce, if not more. You can't afford to send them out unless you know that the maximum possible number of recipients will respond;

3 Between one-third and two-thirds of the products in an average catalogue will break even. Of the rest, half will make you money and the other half will lose money. As soon as you identify the losers, drop them from the catalogue;

4 Remember that many people will return goods. For clothing catalogues, returns can be as high as 60 per cent;

5 A successful catalogue needs a high mark-up on products (usually 50 to 100 per cent) and a high average order value. Keep calculating your average order value – you need to know what it is in order to cost every mailing, and you need to know if it goes up or down, and find out why;

6 Everything we covered in Chapter 3 about image is almost more

important in mail order than anything else. Your company's personality will come through strongly in your catalogue (whether you like it or not), and the recipients will judge from that whether you are 'their kind of company'. They will judge you on your design, the type of paper you use, the style of the text describing the products, and so on. Make sure these fit with your company image. Your image is also doubly important because your customers can't actally see or touch the product itself, or watch it working. So they must have a high level of trust and confidence in you before they will order it;

7 Your writing style is important. Look at other people's catalogues for ideas, but make sure you give a believable description of each product, that highlights at least one or two key benefits. Make your catalogue easy and interesting to read. The style of your writing is a key part of projecting your company personality, so haul those friends of yours out of hiding and ask their opinion;

8 Make sure you give any useful practical information for each product, such as whether the batteries are supplied, or which operating systems the computer software you sell will run under;

9 A good offer will increase your response rate. Something along the lines of *buy two and get one free,* or *a free bucket and spade if you order before 31 March,* or *5 per cent discount on orders over* £50.00;

10 It can take people weeks or even months to respond to a catalogue. Make sure it looks worth keeping.

Designing the catalogue

First, your catalogue must be in full colour throughout. The only exceptions to this are if you are in a line of business where it is standard to print in black and white, such as plant nurseries. (Even so, some print in colour and get a higher response rate.) The same goes for photographs – you must show a photograph of every product. If you cannot afford a catalogue that carries a colour photo of each product, don't go into the mail order business. You'll be throwing your money away on a grand scale.

Having established that point, let's have a look at the most important guidelines for designing your full colour, photo-packed catalogue:

● Go for variety: close up and long distance photographs, three products on one page and eight on the next, an unexpected combination of

products on the page, photos of different sizes. Use headlines and sub-headings to vary and break up the page;
- Average around five products to the page;
- Organise your products in double page spreads, because that's how the reader will view the catalogue. But don't be too obvious about the categories you use, or you remove the element of surprise;
- Use some photographs that include people;
- If you use cut-out photographs of your products against a white (or pale) background, you create a smarter, more upmarket (and more expensive) image than if you use square and rectangular photographs with their own backgrounds;
- The best selling pages – where you should put your best products – are the outside covers, the first double page spread, the first few right hand pages, the centre pages, and the order form.

Designing the order form

- The order form (if there is one) should be idiot-proof. Even so, some people will get confused filling it in, so make it as simple as possible, and then test it on those friends of yours (if they haven't emigrated by now to escape you);
- Design the order form to match the envelope and the letter in quality and style;
- Repeat any special offers on the order form;
- Give people plenty of space and opportunity to order plenty of items, and several of each (include a 'quantity' column);
- Repeat your address on the order form, in case your customer loses the rest of the mailshot;
- Remember that you have to use the order form when it comes back, so make it easy for yourself to follow as well;
- Print some kind of code on the order form so that you can record which mailing the order came from;
- As far as the envelope is concerned, follow the earlier guidelines for how to get people to respond to a direct mail letter.

Be warned, if you are about to start a mail-order operation, that the technicalities of printing catalogues, stock control, order fulfilment and packaging cannot be too carefully planned. Make sure you're ready for all the orders that come in.

Telemarketing

Telemarketing is more than just selling over the telephone. We have already covered selling in Chapter 6, but you can use the telephone for all sorts of other useful purposes as well. As with face-to-face selling, cold calling (selling over the phone when you have initiated the call) encompasses more skills and techniques than I have room to cover here. If you want to use this form of telemarketing – which can be highly effective – I recommend you study the subject in some detail. You'll find there are numerous techniques, but none of them will be beyond you to acquire.

I will say, however, that more and more businesses are taking their sales staff off the road and putting them on the telephone. Telephone selling has two, related advantages over face-to-face selling (where you go to the customer):

1 It is far more cost effective. A sales visit can cost between ten and forty times as much as a phone call;
2 You can speak to far more people. A sales person on the phone can talk to between fifteen and twenty-five top level business decision makers in a day, or over hundred consumers. You wouldn't manage that on the road.

Using the phone to support face-to-face selling

You may feel that you have to be on the road to sell your product; there certainly are some products that people are unlikely to buy unless you visit them. But this doesn't rule out the option of telemarketing altogether. Perhaps you make a regular, quarterly sales visit to each customer. How about visiting them every six months instead, and phoning them in between?

If each visit is costing you £150 (a fairly conservative estimate by the time you've costed in overheads, depreciation on your car and all the rest of it), this will save you £300 in visits. The extra phone calls will cost you perhaps £30 at the most (on the same basis). That's £270 you've saved. And several hours of your time, to spend on visiting new prospects, or making more phone calls. If you're worried about how your customers will react, tell them you're doing it to save *them* time (which it will).

Using the phone to support your mailshots

You can use the phone to increase the response to your mailshots. If you follow up each letter with a phone call, your response rate will (for the average business) increase from around 2 per cent to 15 per cent. If you phone before you mail, your response rate should be between 5 and 15 per cent. And if you phone, then mail, then phone again, you can expect a response of between 10 and 20 per cent. These figures will vary from business to business, so test the effect on a few prospects or customers first and measure how useful the technique is for you.

What are you supposed to say to them? If you call before you mail, simply tell them briefly what the subject of the letter is and ask if you can send them some information. For example, phone round department stores saying 'We manufacture top quality children's garden play equipment, which I think would complement your existing range. Can I send you a brochure?' A few days after you send it (with a covering letter that refers to your phone conversation), call them again. Now you're into a telephone sales call, but with a head start.

If you have thousands of people on your mailing list, don't write this idea off completely. You could use the technique for your key prospects only. Or you might use it to test new mailings, because of the benefits of the feedback you get from speaking to the customer or prospect directly.

You can also use the phone for list cleaning. You may not find it cost effective to phone everyone on your mailing list, but you could make a point of asking them when you speak to them on the phone to confirm their details.

Market research

As we saw in Chapter 2, you can use the phone to call customers, prospects, suppliers, competitors and useful organisations to help you with research. You can have an informal structure, or a specific question to ask, or you can draw up a questionnaire and go through it on the phone.

Dealing with complaints

We have already covered the techniques for complaint handling in Chapter 5. And we have seen how a well-handled complaint can sometimes improve your relationship with the customers and increase their loyalty. The telephone as a route for complaining is an important part of telemarketing. A lot of customers (particularly the younger and middle-aged) prefer to complain over the phone, and you should make sure they have the opportunity to do so. As we saw in Chapter 5, you should clearly publicise a contact phone number on all your literature so that any dissatisfied customer can contact you quickly, and you can put things right for them.

Building customer loyalty

As we've already seen, it can cost between three and seven times more to win new customers than it costs to keep the customers you've already got. And the telephone is an invaluable tool for building a relationship with your customers that makes them want to stay with you.

Phone your customers more often – it really makes a difference to how they view you and your business. I'm not suggesting you pester them on a weekly basis, but a quick phone call every few months makes a world of difference. Let them know you care. Call them after a purchase to check they are happy with their goods. Let them know about a really exciting new product by phone instead of by post. Call to remind them to renew their membership, contract or whatever. Ring to say that they have left it longer than usual before placing an order; are they running low on anything? My chimney sweep (the one who talks too much) rings me every September to remind me that it's that time of year again, and to make an appointment. It's the only reason I don't get round to finding a less garrulous sweep; if I had to dig out a number and make the call myself, I'd call someone else.

It should go without saying that all the guidelines for telephone customer care that we covered in Chapter 5 apply to telemarketing. Make sure that you are consistently friendly and efficient whatever kind of call you are making or receiving.

Did it work?

One of the great joys about direct marketing is that it's terribly easy to answer this question. The whole range of techniques exists precisely in order to be able to judge what works and what doesn't and to feed that information back into the system to make it ever more and more accurate.

The important thing to appreciate is that the time you have to spend keeping your database clean and filling it with information is not wasted. It is one of the most useful ways you can invest your time.

You need to measure the response to everything you can, and keep looking for patterns. Test your hunches. If you think 'That's the third person I've spoken to this week who I haven't heard from in a year', question why. Check out how many of your customers order once a year, or on certain specific dates. Perhaps they buy their child (or each child) a new piece of equipment on their birthday each year? Call and ask them. If you're right, you can record which customers do this, and make a note to send out a catalogue to them a few weeks before the relevant date each year (you could have six catalogue mailing dates a year instead of just one or two).

Direct marketing isn't only a different way of marketing. It is a whole approach to it which will inform all your other marketing activities. The information you gather on your customers and prospects is what helps you to target new prospects, work out which exhibitions to attend, decide which publications to send your press releases to, choose the best type of advertising, and all the rest of it.

Marketing your business gets easier and easier as you go on, because everything you do tells you something useful to apply to the next project, exercise or campaign. All you have to do is listen to what your experience is telling you. Before you know it, you'll be running a thriving company that's well on its way to becoming a larger business. And the smaller companies setting up around you will be coming to you for advice. Just remember to tell them the five rules of marketing your small business:

1 Pretend you're a customer;
2 Set objectives for everything you do;
3 Make your mistakes in your head;
4 Don't try to be too perfect;
5 Know your limitations.

USEFUL ADDRESSES

British Agents Register
24 Mount Parade
Harrogate
North Yorkshire
HG1 1BP
Tel: 01423 560608

Direct Marketing Association
 (UK) Ltd
Haymarket House
1 Oxendon Street
London
SW1Y 4EE
Tel: 0171 321 2525

Federation of Small Businesses
32 Orchard Road
Lytham St Anne's
Lancashire
FY8 1NY
Tel: 01253 720911

Manufacturers' Agents Association
1 Somers Road
Reigate
Surrey
RH2 9DU
Tel: 01737 241025

Data Protection Registrar
Springfield House
Water Lane
Wilmslow
Cheshire
SK9 5AX

Exhibition Bulletin
272 Kirkdale
London
SE26 4RZ
Tel: 0181 778 2288

Mail Order Protection Scheme
16 Took's Court
London
EC4A 1LB
Tel: 0171 405 6806

National Federation of Enterprise
 Agencies
c/o Cadbury Schweppes plc
Bournville D24
Birmingham
B30 2LU
Tel: 0121 458 2000, extension 3955

INDEX